PLAY BETTER SQUASH

PLAY BETTER SQUASH

John Beddington

Macdonald
Queen Anne Press

A *Queen Anne Press* BOOK

© John Beddington 1974, 1977 and 1984

First published in 1974
Second edition 1977
Third edition 1984
Reprinted 1987

Published by
Queen Anne Press, a division of
Macdonald & Co (Publishers) Ltd,
3rd Floor, Greater London House,
Hampstead Road, London NW1 7QX

A BPCC plc Company

Front cover: Hiddy Jahan and Jahanghir Khan (*All-Sport*)

Back cover: Gawain Briars (*Colorsport*)

Beddington, John
    Play better squash. — New ed.
    1. Squash rackets (Game)
    I. Title
    796.34'3   GV1004

ISBN 0-356-10584-9
ISBN 0-356-10585-7 Pbk

Typeset by Cylinder Typesetting Ltd, London

Printed and bound in Great Britain by
Hazell Watson & Viney Limited,
Member of the BPCC Group,
Aylesbury, Bucks

CONTENTS

Foreword

by Jonah Barrington

It is fitting that the game of squash and my old friend John Bedding-ton have travelled well. Since his thoughts in the mid-seventies about the development of the sport in *Play Better Squash*, so much has happened and an enormous number of new participants both in the UK and overseas have been introduced to the eternal subtleties and mysteries of the game.

John himself, after attaining a very sound and shrewd proficiency as an exponent, became involved in the construction and direction of squash courts – the first promoter of an international squash circuit on a level theretofore not considered practical – and inevitably advanced into varied and successful entrepreneurial endeavours in North America.

Much, of course, has changed – it seems only yesterday that I was battling against opponents hell-bent on taking away my title. The cruellest adversary, anno domini, rapidly and stealthily sealed my fate. Geoffrey Hunt, the great Australian, then bestrode the squash world, fighting off the pack with breathtaking persist-ence until even his time came, as it had to, and the prodigy Jahangir stole the crown away. Time does indeed fly but the game itself remains the same, a marvellous constant and tribute to its originators.

Selfishly I have always felt that my sport at the highest competi-tive plane would have evolved faster and commercially much better had John Beddington remained with us and not set out for new mountains to climb. I find it enormously pleasing that his book, *Play Better Squash*, is now revised and updated. It is, and always will be, a most excellent and comprehensive summation of the essentials of squash, and is as relevant in this and any other decade just as it was in the 'boom' years of the seventies.

Foreword to the First Edition

by Rex Bellamy, Tennis and Squash Correspondent of *The Times* and author of books on tennis, squash and hill climbing.

A long association with tennis and squash has, among other advantages, granted me the privilege and pleasure of a close acquaintance with three congenial JBs: John Barrett in tennis, Jonah Barrington in squash, and John Beddington in both. All are energetically imaginative and have a rare capacity for opening windows in the mind. John Beddington, the author of this popular book, is the least well known of the three because his talents have primarily been exercised on the periphery of the courts rather than in the spotlight of personal publicity. But his relatively modest status as a player is, in this case, a recommendation: because he is writing mainly for his would-be peers in the higher echelons of club squash, for those who are facing, or are about to face, the kind of challenges he has met and mastered himself.

He was never taught squash, but picked up the game at Eton and subsequently reached a high level as a club player. That is probably more than most of his readers will achieve. But it represents a standard to which all can reasonably aspire if they have the ambition, ability, and character. This book helps them on the way because it is written by a man who understands their problems and is still young enough to share them. During the past I have played the author not only at his own club (a relaxed rendezvous for players at every level) but also, by a bizarre combination of circumstances, in Manhattan and at Salem in Massachusetts. His experience of American squash indicates an unquenchable enthusiasm for the game, no matter where or how it may be played.

His wide-ranging interests made him a director of the Lambton Squash Club in London, and the Top Squash Club in Frankfurt as well as European Tennis Director for the Grand Prix circuit and its climactic Masters tournament. He created and organised the World Series of Squash, the first coordinated international circuit of squash tournaments. He is recognised as one of the foremost Tennis and Squash Tournament Directors in the world. That in the midst of all this he found time to write an admirable and successful book on squash is at once remarkable and typical.

The bulk of this volume concerns tactics and technique. But there is also much solid information and sensible comment on wide areas of the game. The author is always good company and his readers benefit from the advice of a kindred spirit. They may also find future comfort in the fact that, if there are no squash courts in the next world, John Beddington is the kind of man who will build some.

Acknowledgements

Inevitably there are many people to whom an acknowledgement should be addressed with reference to this book. Equally inevitable is the fact that they cannot all be mentioned.

Knowledge gained in any subject, especially in a sport such as squash, is the result of many years experience, both on and off court – mine is no exception. I have been lucky enough to meet many people interested in the game, including the world's top players, administrators and enthusiasts. Most of these friends and acquaintances have contributed to this book, however indirectly, for my knowledge and enthusiasm for this superb game have been increased by contact with them.

In writing this book, I received invaluable advice from my wife Roseann, who does not play squash but who patiently and laboriously typed the manuscript, improving it in the process. I would also like to thank the following for their help and encouragement in revising the text for this edition: Andrew Shelley of the Squash Rackets Association in London for his help in revising some of the sections; Tom and Hazel Jones of *Squash News* in New York, North America's leading squash publication; Jane Wynne and Howard Seto in Toronto and Sylvie Asselin in Montreal.

No acknowledgement would be complete without mentioning the players. Particular thanks go to Gogi Alauddin, Hiddy Jahan and Qamar Zaman, while no book on squash is complete without acknowledgement to Jonah Barrington's contribution.

I thank Rex Bellamy, who writes so fluently for *The Times* on both tennis and squash, for his original foreword, and Jonah Barrington for writing the foreword to this new edition.

Introduction

So you want to play squash? Well, this book has been written not only for the beginner learning to play for the first time, but also for the player who has been hitting the ball around for some time and wants to improve his present standard.

For the beginner the first sight of a squash court may be daunting. The view from the gallery is of a more or less square, gleaming pit with wooden floor, white walls and ceiling, no windows, and apparently no door. The first sight of squash being played may, of course, be equally disconcerting – two men dressed in white shirts, shorts, shoes, and socks running wildly to and fro whacking a little black ball around the walls with alarming enthusiasm.

However, the beginner can quickly appreciate the enjoyment to be gained from the game. The physical activity, the need for fast reflexes, and the concentration and anticipation make squash a superb fun and exercise game. For the more advanced player, improvement will bring ample opportunity for tournament and championship match play at all levels, from club ladders and leagues to international status.

It had been said that becoming a champion is, like genius, the result of 90 per cent perspiration and 10 per cent inspiration. Squash is a game that exercises both the mind and the body, so that any effort to improve needs to be both mental and physical. However, to become a real champion at the game, the perspiration will be more of the mind than the body. Physical fitness is vital, but it is a small matter by comparison with the mental effort the average player must make for consistent improvement.

The popularity of squash has increased beyond all expectation during the past few years, largely because it is a game suitable for both men and women of all ages – from those still at school to those approaching, or even well into, middle-age. It has also become the most cosmopolitan game of our time.

Traditionally, books on sport are written by experts, for example, Rod Laver on tennis, or Jack Nicklaus on golf. This book is about squash – what the game is and how it is played. Above all, it is a game to be played with enthusiasm – and in that respect this book is written by an expert. Although there are countless squash players who are better than I am, there are few who take more pleasure in the game.

Part One

1 SO YOU WANT TO PLAY SQUASH?

It had taken a lot of persuading. After all, James had not taken any form of exercise for three years and it had begun to show. His muscles, once proud and taut, were in an early stage of flabbiness and his waistline was not quite what it used to be. Not quite a paunch – he was only 28 – but perhaps his friends were right. Squash might be the answer for him. It seemed to be popular with many people.

James's real problem was not fear of fierce exercise but fear of being ineffectual, which would severely damage his pride. In his earlier years he had kept quite fit and managed to be fairly competent at athletic games, but he would be a complete beginner at squash. Some of his friends at the office had played for years and their enthusiasm, to say nothing of their apparent fitness, was daunting. He did not particularly relish the thought of losing to any of them.

But the fight had been won. One cold winter's night James found himself setting off for his first game of squash. He had searched around in his wardrobe and found his old tennis shoes which had turned a distinctive yellow. He added a white holiday shirt and some white football shorts, that were very tight round the waist, and he was off, both nervous and excited, yet at the same time pleased that he had finally made the effort.

The squash club was pleasant and comfortable and his opponent greeted him cheerfully, with no hint of embarrassment at the strange assortment of sports gear that appeared from James's bag. James was not completely ignorant of the game – he remembered that it wasn't very different from tennis in some ways. One player serves, the other player returns, and the rally continues until one of the players makes a mistake. Instead of being on opposite sides of the court, squash opponents must share the same confined space, and instead of hitting the ball 'over the net' it must be hit above a line on the front wall of the court. Squash couldn't be too difficult as it therefore consists of hitting a ball around in a four-walled room. Shots must be easier to make, as it is quite difficult to hit a ball out of a four-walled room – in tennis it is easy to send it too far or too wide.

James's opponent kindly lent him a squash racket, and he soon found himself on court about to begin the knock-up. His friendly opponent had chosen a very slow ball and James was somewhat taken aback to find that it hardly bounced at all – it merely plopped against the wall and refused to return to the back of the court. But James was quick to learn that the ball must be warmed up, and that the best way to do this is to hit it as hard as possible at the front wall. So, with a swing of the racket and on flat feet, James began. He was pleasantly surprised at how simple it seemed to hit the ball at the wall, and, having realised that the wall is a vast area offering a great margin for error, he began to find squash less frightening. However, he had already begun to make mistakes that would be harder to rectify the longer they persisted.

James soon found that being able to hit the ball, he could begin to play a game. A quick discussion of the basic rules and the determination of someone who hates to lose soon enabled him to perform with reasonable competence. At the beginning, the pace of his improvement was his greatest encouragement; but after a while, although his enthusiasm remained and the will to practise strengthened, nothing more was achieved in terms of progress. It was at this point that James realised that he had improved as much as possible on his erratic beginning to the game and if he was going to improve any further he would need help. Furthermore, he was going to have to unlearn some of the faulty techniques he had developed.

Where could he go for help? Coaching is available from several sources, but is often expensive and inaccessible. However, a few books exist on the basic technical approach to the game – this is another one! The idea that a book can teach anyone to play a game is debatable, but many fine sportsmen as well as ordinary club players use books and articles to learn more about their own sport.

Squash is one of the obvious games to be learnt from a book for two very good reasons. It is not a difficult sport to begin, as James discovered, and there seems little reason why it should be a difficult sport to learn *correctly* once one has begun. Simple instructional passages on the basic strokes can be easily followed and put into practice. The other principal reason stems from the extreme shortage of qualified professional coaches; the game has expanded so fast that the increasing demand for coaching at all levels has far exceeded the supply of coaches. Consequently the majority of beginners must learn the first steps with the aid of a book.

Looking at the state of another increasingly popular game, golf, one beginner seeking professional advice on how to take it up was told to find a 'basic swing', and then practise for six months before venturing on to the course. There is much to be said for this type of advice if the player in question has the determination of an Olympic athlete. Unfortunately most beginners have not, and so this book is not aimed at Olympic athlete types. The desire to improve is tempered by an eagerness to play matches. To be locked on a squash court for six months until one can hit the ball with unerring efficiency is perhaps the quickest way to improve, but it is certainly not the most enjoyable.

Play Better Squash aims to help the beginner, whatever his ambitions, to play properly right from the start. He can still play matches and it is hoped that he will; but if he follows the instructional sections, he will adopt the correct techniques and tactics in a simple progression, until he finds to his great surprise that he is playing good squash. That is not to say that poor James has been left in an anguished plight. The book will show him his errors, and on the strength of his own ability he will be able to rebuild a sound platform from which to improve.

That is what learning a new game means – the building of a sound technique that will not falter whatever the stresses and pressures applied to it. Allied to this comes a basic understanding of what can be achieved and of what the player is trying to achieve, whether during a particularly close game or during his career as a whole. It is hoped that this book will be of value not only to the beginner or to the moderate player; for if by its very simplicity it reminds the better player of some of the fundamentals of the game of squash, then it will be of help to him also.

The Game of Squash Rackets

The game of singles in squash is played between two players. One player serves the ball from one of the two service boxes on to the front wall above the service or cut line and below the boundary line, so that it rebounds into the opposite back quarter of the court behind the short line and on the other side of the half-court line. The server is known as *hand in* and the receiver is known as *hand out*. The right to serve at the beginning of a game is decided by the spin of a racket.

After the server (hand in) has served, the receiver (hand out) can return the ball by hitting it after it has bounced on the floor, or on the volley before it bounces. Whichever option he chooses, the ball must be returned, without bouncing on the floor either directly or by way of one of the other walls, to the front wall above the board or tin.

From that point, players hit the ball alternately and play continues until one of them fails to make a good return. This can happen if he does not reach the ball before it bounces on the floor for the second time, or if he hits the ball below the board into the tin or above the boundary line on any of the four walls. It is also possible to lose a point by standing in the path of an opponent's ball if it would have travelled directly to the front wall after he has hit it.

If a player has been hand in and loses a rally, he loses the right to serve and the hand out receiver becomes hand in as server. Points can be scored only by the server, and if a rally is won by the

15

Diagram 1a The court: definitions.

receiver, the serve changes hands but no point is scored.

The first player to reach nine points wins the game unless the score reaches eight-all. If this happens, the receiver has the choice of playing one more point or two, to nine points or 10. Thus a game can be won 10-8, 9-8, or 10-9, depending on this choice. Matches are usually the best of five games, the winner being the player who is first to win three games.

This is a brief summary of how squash is played and the further you read the more you will understand. A beginner will soon notice the attractions of the game: plenty of exercise in a short period and in a fairly limited area; unlike tennis or badminton, the margin of error in hitting the ball out of court is considerable – it is therefore easier to keep the rally going and requires less basic skill to be able to play at all; squash can be practised on your own without the absolute necessity of a partner or opponent (improvement is also more likely to follow from practising alone as far as technique is concerned); squash is invigorating.

Squash does not damage your ability or skill in other sports such as tennis. There are several very good tennis players and other sports celebrities who are also more than just proficient at squash. They use squash as a training ground for other sports since it requires sharp reflexes, breathing, speed, accuracy, and coordination.

Now let us move on to the technical requirements of the game.

Equipment and Clothing

Apart from the basic necessity of a court in which to play, the equipment and clothing required for playing squash can be readily obtained at any reasonable sports, or club professional's, shop. Finding a court is less easy and, when located, they are usually heavily booked in advance. A list of affiliated clubs in your area can be obtained from the Squash Rackets Association, Francis House, Francis Street, London, SW1P 1DE. The whereabouts of public courts can usually be obtained from the appropriate local authority.

The basic equipment for squash is a racket and ball; the basic clothing includes shirt, shorts, socks, and shoes. Women can replace the shirt and shorts with a dress suitable for sport or a shirt and skirt. These items need not be expensive and you may find that you already have some of them if you play tennis. One important fact to remember is that the rules of the game stipulate that all clothing should be white. The reason for this is that a black ball can be sighted more easily when crossing a white surface. Some people feel that the all-white rule may be changed in deference to colour television but it is expected that this will be only for televised play, if at all.

The Racket

The choice of a racket depends on the individual, who must first decide upon the price range he can afford. Racket prices vary enormously, and for the beginner a modestly-priced one is quite sufficient. The head of the racket must have a wooden frame but the shaft may be made of wood, metal, cane, or even glass-fibre.

The important point to remember about choosing a racket is that it should feel comfortable – the weight and the balance must suit the individual. The grip on the handle is also a matter of personal choice, and may be either towelling or leather. Towelling grips have a short life but are inexpensive and easily replaceable. They are recommended for those who find leather grips slippery. One can even buy rackets with grips moulded to the pattern of the hand so that the beginner is sure to hold the racket in the correct way.

It does not matter to the beginner if the racket is strung with gut or synthetic fibres. However, experienced players may find that rackets strung with gut provide more control. (Nylon and other synthetic strings have a longer life, are cheaper and more easily obtained, while gut strings become scarcer and as a result more expensive.) The racket should be treated carefully, particularly if strung with gut. Do not leave it with wet clothes as the gut will fray quickly in damp conditions. It is not essential to use a press with modern rackets, a plastic headcover being quite satisfactory. The racket should be left in a dry and cool place.

If you are to play in a match and some of the strings in your racket are slightly frayed, it is better to have the strings repaired beforehand, rather than having to interrupt the match when a string breaks. One other point to remember; however good or expensive a racket is, it will not last any longer than any other if it is hit hard enough against the walls or the floor.

The Ball

The ball and the racket are both defined in the final section of this book.

In the United kingdom, there are four types of what is basically the same ball – blue dot, red dot, white dot, and yellow dot. The blue dot is the fastest and the yellow dot is the slowest. It is the yellow dot that is used in tournaments and competitive events.

The speed of the ball varies not only because of its own specification but also on account of the type of court on which it is used. On a hot court the air inside the ball warms up with the result that the ball moves off the walls faster. Therefore, it is obviously better to use a slow ball on a fast or hot court, and a faster ball on a slow or cold court. Apart from using the type of ball most suitable for the court on which you are playing, it is generally easier for the beginner to start with a fast or blue dot ball.

Shoes

There are many different varieties of shoe that can be used for squash, but a basic white canvas one with a good gripping sole is quite satisfactory as long as it is strong enough to cope with the pressures put on it by constant twisting and turning. The shoe must not have black soles which will mark the court's surface.

When buying shoes, bear in mind the thickness and number of pairs of socks you will wear.

Socks

It is most important that your feet feel comfortable when you are wearing socks and shoes, otherwise you will not be able to concentrate on your game.

Some players wear no socks, while others wear one or even two pairs. It is usually advisable and comfortable to wear some, but however many pairs you wear depends on your individual comfort. If your feet blister easily then you may prefer to wear two pairs, though usually one thick pair is enough. The prime importance is comfort.

Always wear a clean pair of socks each time you play; apart from anything else, dirty socks cause blisters more easily. Look after your feet – wash and dry them carefully after playing; and use foot powder if you feel it necessary.

Shirts, shorts, skirts, dresses etc.

These clothes should be white, easily washable, and, most important, comfortable. They should not be too tight or too loose, or restricting in any way.

Other Equipment

Other useful items for the squash player include a towel, which is essential and should be available outside the court for use between games. Towelling wristlets can be useful for the player who finds sweat pouring down his arms an unnecessary danger to a firm grip on the racket.

Sweatbands came into use originally to aid the player with glasses. Fewer people play in glasses now that contact lenses are available, but sweatbands are still useful for keeping long hair under control.

A wide variety of sports bags are available in which to carry your clothing and equipment.

It may seem unnecessary to go into such detail on equipment and clothing as much of what has been said may seem obvious. However, it is necessary to stress the importance of these aspects of the game and also how preferable it is to have your own. Keep it in good condition and turn up on court looking well prepared in clean clothes. The advantage in doing so may be psychological – but it will be an advantage nevertheless.

Diagram 1b The court: dimensions.

The Court

How the size of a court became standardized is described in 'The state of the game'. The standard dimensions of a squash court are defined in the last section of the book. However, there are still many courts that have not been built to the standard international dimensions. These are either relics of the time when there was no standard specification for a court, or those which have been built since then without due consultation with the experts.

A court is basically 32 feet from the back wall to the front wall and 21 feet across. The diagram on the facing page shows the dimensions. The walls of the court should be white and constructed of a special type of hard plaster which has to contend with considerable wear and tear.

The floor should be well sprung and ideally made of maple, but other strong timber, such as pine or birch, may be used. However, the floor must not be treated with too much seal; this will make it very slippery, because sweat will not be absorbed, and dangerous accidents may be caused.

The board or tin (or 'tell-tale' as it is sometimes known) is set at the bottom of the front wall, and should have a small cupboard set into it in which to place wallets, watches, handbags, and other valuables during a game.

The ceiling should have a clearance well above the specification in the rules and a minimum of 19 feet is suggested for good squash. Also, the lights should not hang down so far that they will impede high shots but should be set high in the ceiling to illuminate the court brightly and evenly.

A gallery is not imperative, but is useful for spectators. If the court is a cold one, some form of heating in the gallery is recommended as squash can otherwise be an extremely cold game to watch.

One important aspect of any squash court or set of courts is ventilation. Without proper ventilation, walls will sweat and condensation will form.

These are just a few points about the court which may serve as a guide. However, the business of constructing a squash court is highly technical and, if you are ever considering it, you must seek advice from the experts at the SRA. Short cuts in construction are usually a false economy, since mistakes can be very expensive to rectify. If the builder is unfamiliar with court construction, check with the SRA on plans and construction materials. The SRA will also be able to guide you on the best types of floor or plaster and so on.

2 ELEMENTARY STROKES

The Grip

At this stage, we must assume that you are familiar with the basic principle of squash. There are two players on the court and you are taking turns at hitting the ball and in so doing trying to frustrate the efforts of your opponent in making a good return (without actually standing in his way). Thus, reduced to simplicity, your object is to strike the ball against the front wall and cause it to bounce twice on the floor before your opponent can produce a reply to your shot. If you do that you win a point, and if you do it often enough you will win enough points to win the game, and eventually the match.

Your shot will be made either as a defensive measure against your opponent's attack, or as an offensive measure to put your opponent on the defensive. It is important that you should understand this distinction now, because once you are on court playing, the difference between the two will be forgotten while you are more concerned with the problems of reaching the ball and hitting it effectively.

It is important to emphasize that learning to strike the ball correctly on both the forehand and backhand sides is absolutely essential. There are no short cuts and practice is the only way to achieve a satisfactory and fluent consistency of stroke. So the first thing to learn is how to grip the racket properly, in order to be able to hit the ball most effectively. Squash is a game that demands a high degree of efficiency; consequently you must ensure that the first step is an entirely correct foundation on which to build your game. If you are a beginner and you do not learn to grip the racket in the right way at the outset, it will be extremely difficult for you to readjust later.

However, every squash player, being human, is different – there are no two Jahanghir Khans and you must allow your own natural tendencies to be moulded into your style of play, so that you do not limit your horizons. This individuality applies to the grip as much as to the rest of your game. We will show you the conventional grip here but players with unorthodox ones have been known to be equally successful.

With the first purposeful wrapping of the fingers round the racket handle comes your initiation into the wonderful game of squash. Take the racket in your left hand (if you are right-handed) and hold it vertically by the shaft with the racket face facing sideways. Extend your right hand to 'shake hands' with the racket handle, and settle your thumb and forefinger round it with the 'V' on top. The palm of the hand is slightly behind the handle and the other fingers are spread round it to give support and solidity. The

Diagram 2 The grip. Note that (A) the thumb is placed between forefinger and second finger, while (B) the V between thumb and forefinger is almost central on the handle.

thumb should extend round the handle, ending up between the forefinger and the second finger. Some experts prefer to advise gripping the handle like a hammer, and if you prefer this then the forefinger should meet the thumb round it (but on the inside).

The 'V' formed by the thumb and forefinger should be almost central on the centre line of the shaft of the racket but slightly to the right. The racket should be held as near to the base of the handle as is comfortable.

Once you have settled your hand round the handle in this way, swing the racket round for a few minutes to get the feel of it. Do not hold it too tightly – it is not necessary. Your grip should be relaxed and should only be tightened for hitting the ball. If you hold the racket tightly the whole time, the strain will begin to make itself felt and your arm will tire more quickly.

The Forehand Drive
Apart from the serve there are four basic strokes in squash: the drive, the lob, the drop, and the angle. All other shots are variations of these (except the volley) and all of them can be played either on the forehand or the backhand. On these strokes depends the entire structure of the game and your endeavour must be to hit with maximum effect and minimum effort. Now that you have adopted

Diagram 3 The forehand: (A) backswing (B) impact (C) follow through. Note that the weight is transferred from right foot to left.

a grip that gives you the greatest allowance for the free execution of these strokes, the path ahead should be easier.

The first and most important shot to learn is the drive, the basic weapon in the armoury of the beginner. Remembering from James's experience that it is not enough to hit the ball hard, you must learn to hit it with consistency and control, qualities more important than sheer strength. This is also a good moment to mention what may seem obvious – keep your eye on the ball. Many mistakes are made by average players who do not watch the ball right on to the racket.

The drive can be divided into three parts; backswing and preparation, impact, and follow-through. With your left foot forward and your feet at right angles to the side wall, you are standing parallel to the course of your shot. Your weight should start on the right foot as you raise the racket on the backswing to a point just above and behind your head. The elbow should remain bent and the wrist should remain cocked so that the racket head is held up vertically.

Your knees should be bent at this stage as you will be able to move the weight of your body more easily from right foot to left foot. The more weight you put into a shot the more powerful it will be. Swing the racket down from the backswing position above and behind your right shoulder and simultaneously shift the weight of your body to the front foot, keeping the knee bent for balance. Strike the ball at a point just opposite your front foot and parallel to the front wall, keeping your shoulders square to the side wall. Be careful not to let your shoulders turn until the ball has been struck and your follow-through has begun. If your shoulders open towards the front wall before impact the ball will tend to fly off across the court instead of up and down. This usually stems from a desire to hit the ball too hard and should be avoided until you have worked your forehand drive into a well-grooved stroke.

The racket should follow through continuing its arc to a point above the left shoulder, with the elbow slightly bent so that the racket stays close to the body.

The action of hitting the ball is similar to throwing one. Although the wrist should remain cocked during the backswing, it may be lowered for the moment of impact depending on the height at which the ball will be struck.

You should learn the forehand and backhand drives with the racket-face square to the front wall; do not attempt at this stage to use spin, or to cut the ball, as mistakes can easily be made. It is more important to become proficient at the basic strokes before learning sophisticated variations.

The Backhand Drive
To many beginners, the backhand stroke may seem more difficult than the forehand, but this should not be so – after all, it is easier to throw a hat at a hat-rack with a backhand swing rather than a forehand. Beginners who spend more time practising the supposedly more difficult backhand often end up with a more fluent and correct stroke than on the forehand, where the initial swing at the ball may tend to prevail because it has met with reasonable success. The backhand is an instinctive stroke.

The basic ingredients of the backhand drive are similar to those of the forehand, except that the ball falls on the player's opposite side. For instance, if the player is right-handed and the ball falls on his right as he faces the front wall, he will play a forehand; if it falls on the left, he will play a backhand. As squash is played within walls it is not often possible to run round a backhand and hit it on the forehand as can be done in tennis or badminton.

Once again it is necessary to emphasize that the proper execution of the stroke should be learnt. The wrist and the forearm should follow a sweeping arc down from a high but compact backswing, with the arc from left to right. There should be no inward turning of the wrist.

As the racket sweeps down to the ball, the moment of impact corresponds to the moment at which you let go of the hat towards

Diagram 4 The backhand: (A) backswing (B) impact (C) follow through.
Note that the weight is transferred from left foot to right.

the hat-rack, and is similar to slapping with the back of the hand. However, the fact that the backhand is more instinctive than the forehand does not mean that you will necessarily end up with a stronger backhand stroke. Each individual player will use his own method, adapting the textbook stroke. This is merely to show you the ease with which you will be able to pick up the technique for the backhand.

Thus the stroke itself will start from above the left shoulder with the weight on the back (left) foot. The wrist remains cocked and the racket head up, with the right shoulder at right angles to the front wall. Maintain a well-balanced stance while you transfer your weight to the front foot as the racket begins its sweep down to the ball, smacking the ball level with the front foot as the full weight of the body reaches that foot. The knees remain bent and the racket follows through with elbow slightly bent, to keep the racket close to the body.

The Crosscourt Drive
As we have said, the basic forehand and backhand drives just described are the first and most important in a player's armoury of strokes. The straight drive should be played up and down the court parallel with the side wall until you have a well-grooved stroke and

Diagram 5a Straight forehand and backhand drives.

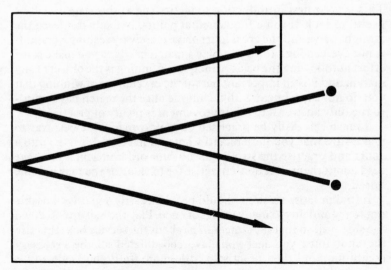

Diagram 5b Crosscourt forehand and backhand drives.

27

swing. When you have practised this on both flanks and feel you have mastered in part the essentials of timing and technique, then we can look at the next stage of the drive – across the court.

The crosscourt drive from the forehand side should be made in a similar way to the forehand drive down the wall. With the front foot forward and the knees bent you should swing the racket back, bending the elbow, and 'throw' the racket at the ball hitting through it. The moment of impact should be in front of the left foot so that you hit the ball early by comparison with the drive down the wall. It is better to keep the racket face open for the crosscourt stroke unless you wish to 'kill' the ball, in which case you will take it at the height of its bounce, stroking down and across. If you do not want to hit the ball in the early position, the same shot can be effected by changing the position of the body so that it is parallel to the path of the stroke you are about to make.

The backhand crosscourt drive should be played in the same way as the forehand but from the left side of the court hitting towards the right. Crosscourt strokes can be used to deceive the opponent – and the art of making your opponent think the ball is going to be hit in a different direction plays a big part in squash. By shaping up for a forehand or a backhand drive, you can hit down the wall or across court merely by changing the moment of impact very slightly. If you hit the ball opposite the front foot it will travel parallel to the body, if you hit it just in front of the front foot it will travel across the court.

Simple Practice
This is your first introduction to tactics and at this stage it will be useful to look at some fundamental points. Nobody can learn the straight drive and the crosscourt drive merely by reading a book. It is not even enough to go and play a match in which you make some effort at following the basic principles. Winning is the object of any match, and it is an important part of the psychology of winning that you do not experiment with technique once the match has begun – so the only answer for real improvement is plenty of practice.

Squash can easily be practised on your own and the best way to make sure that you understand what you have read is to go into a court and practise the strokes in the same order in which you have read about them. But don't practise for too long or you may become bored.

Initial practise sessions should be taken easily and it is advisable not to try and do too many things at once. Play the ball up and down the side wall so that it bounces in or about the service box. Practise the shot until you feel you have coordinated all the necessary technique, and then practise a little more until you begin to hit every ball into the service box.

A good drive is the result of a ball hit at the correct pace and height. To take this one stage further, the most important drive is the one that is hit down the wall to bounce well before the back wall, with the second bounce dying on the back wall. The use of the wall is important, as we shall see in the next section, to prevent your opponent from being able to cut the ball off before it passes him to land at the back of the court.

The length of the drive is an important element in the effectiveness of the shot. If the length is good your opponent will only have one chance to hit it and that is before it passes him. It should not bounce off the back wall to give him a second chance. If the shot is close enough to the wall then your opponent may also be unable to stop the ball before it passes him.

In practising, the whole height of the front wall should be used to gauge the power and direction of your shots. The higher you hit the ball at the front wall, the softer it should be, but you can hit harder as you aim lower towards the tin. If you practise with this in mind then you will soon learn that you do not have to hit the ball too hard all the time. Concentrate all the time while you are practising, for bad practice is worse than none at all.

Practise the crosscourt shots in the same way – aim to hit the ball into the service box area to begin with, and then extend this by aiming to land the ball deep into the far corner from where your opponent will have difficulty in retrieving it.

This elementary tactic of trying to keep the ball away from your opponent will be discussed more fully together with other simple tactics later in this chapter under the heading *Basic Tactics*. Before we get to that stage we must first have a look at the service and the return of the service.

The Service

As every point must begin with a service, you cannot do more than practise without it. It is therefore the only shot which is played in every rally, and it must be included in this chapter before you begin to play a game of any kind.

There are players at all levels who do not pay enough attention to the art of the service. Being the only shot in the game that is not a return of your opponent's shot, you are not in any sense under pressure. You should not consider it as just a method of putting the ball in play and starting a point. It is a good opportunity to put your opponent under pressure even though it is extremely hard to gain a point outright with a service winner.

Having seen that the service can and should be used as an offensive shot, you must use the advantage it will give you. As we will see in the section on tactics, the art of squash is to be able to place the ball where your opponent will find it hardest to retrieve

Diagram 6a The forehand service from the right court: only one foot need be inside the box. The shaded area shows where the ball must bounce.

Diagram 6b The forehand service from the left court: the left foot is nearest to the front wall. The shaded area shows where the ball must bounce.

30

and return. We must now look at how we can put this theory into practice as far as the service is concerned.

For the beginner it will be wise to concentrate on the forehand service from both service boxes. Nearly all players prefer the forehand service although the backhand serve can be used to good effect if only to vary the way in which your opponent has to receive it. There is certainly a case for the backhand serve in the forehand court – this will enable you to keep your eye on your opponent and his movements. However, we will concentrate on the forehand serve for the moment.

There are two principal types of service in squash – the lob and the hard service. The most common and most effective of these (if correctly hit) is the lob, which we will look at first.

Don't forget that you have plenty of time – use it to position yourself correctly. The left foot should be in front of the right, whichever side you serve from, and should be nearer to the front wall. You can stand with either one or both feet in the service box but you will save yourself some movement after you have served if you stand with only one foot firmly in the box. Diagrams 6a and 6b show the ideal position of feet for the forehand serve. Dig your feet in solidly and stand well balanced.

The ball can be hit at any point of the wide arc which extends from your feet to above your head when your racket arm is extended. However, it is better to strike the ball from a position somewhere between knee and shoulder level and preferably at about hip level. The ball should be hit from behind and below in an upward arc which will carry it firmly towards the front wall. The moment of impact should be above the front foot.

You should aim to hit the front wall a little more than halfway across the court and about midway between the cut line and the top boundary line. In your mind you should mark off the area on the front wall at which to aim – an area about four feet high and six feet wide is recommended (as in diagram 7).

The ball should continue to rise, as high as the ceiling permits, on its journey towards the opposite court and should glance off the side wall on its downward path at a point equidistant from the back wall and the floor – preferably between four and six feet. Height is important, as the higher the ball goes in the arc after hitting the front wall, the more vertically it will drop in the far corner. The aim of the lob serve is to keep the ball so close to and high on the side wall that your opponent cannot volley it before it drops.

The ball should drop after hitting the side wall and bounce before hitting the back wall. The only way for your opponent to return this type of serve is by digging it out defensively which keeps you on the offensive and well placed.

Thus the lob service is a carefully hit lob aimed to drop as deep as

31

Area into which ball should be hit

6ft (2m)

4ft (1.2m)

A

B

Diagram 7 The lob service: the ball, hit from the service box, should rebound from the front wall on to the side wall (at A, approx 4-5ft from the back wall, and then bounce (at B) before striking the back wall.

possible in the far corner without your opponent being able to make a good return. If the ball hits the side wall and then the back wall before bouncing it will be forced out into the centre of the court, where your opponent can return it with interest, so try not to overhit the service, or to hit the serve too low so that your opponent can reach it to volley before or after it hits the side wall. You must also avoid hitting the side wall too early as that will bring the ball out into the court as well.

As soon as you have served you should move to the T, the junction of the half-court line and the short line. This is the commanding position in a squash court and you should attempt to reach there before your opponent. (See section on simple tactics.) Remember one thing about the lob service – no power or speed is required, just technique, which can only come from considerable practice.

If your opponent seems to be able to read your serves satisfactorily then you should vary them. This could be the time for you to try a backhand serve to alter the angle at which the ball comes off the front wall. The occasional variation in service may catch your opponent off guard, and surprise can often produce dividends. If your opponent is caught out of position he may have to do a block return or move in the opposite direction to that which he intended.

One of the best ways to catch your opponent in this way is to throw in the occasional hard service, the other principal type of serve. This should be hit from a similar position to the lob service. The ball should be hit flat and aimed hard just above the cut line; it should stay close to the side wall, hitting it close to the floor. The length of the shot should be good, i.e. the second bounce should die on the back wall.

The principles of serving outlined here apply equally to a serve from either side of the court.

Before moving on to the return of service, let us look briefly at the requirements for a service as far as the rules of squash are concerned. When serving, at least one foot must be completely inside the service box (not touching the red line) and the ball must be hit between the cut line and the boundary line on the front wall. Hitting the lines in squash is 'out' and therefore the ball must hit between those two lines. If you do not have one foot completely in the service box it will be counted as a fault. If the ball hits the wall on or below the cut line but above the tin it is a fault; however, your opponent may accept this service by returning it in the normal way which negates the fault.

The ball must also land in the opposite back quarter of the court (the shaded area in diagrams 6a and 6b). If it does not land in that quarter it is also a single fault, but your opponent may accept it by returning it. If you have served a fault, you are allowed another serve but you can only serve twice in this way on each point. Your opponent may also volley the serve before it lands in his quarter.

Double faults are served if you hit the ball on or above the boundary line or on or below the tin on the front wall and also if your serve never reaches the front wall. It is also a double fault if the ball is served and hits the ceiling or the boundary line (or higher) on any of the other three walls. A double fault also occurs if the server serves two single faults, or if he fails to strike the ball at all while attempting to serve. Finally, it is a double fault if the serve touches one of the side walls before the front wall.

Return of Service

After a service, the receiver must return the ball on to the front wall above the tin. Like all other shots, the ball must not touch his body or clothing and must not be hit twice. Unlike the service, the return may hit a side or back wall on its journey to the front wall, where it must land below the boundary line and above the tin. If it does touch a side wall it must do so below the boundary line.

The object of explaining to you how to return the service is simple. It may not be as easy as a straightforward drive and it is important that you learn how to tackle the service from the receiver's

Diagram 8 Receiving service: in left court *above*, in right court *below*. Stand at A, facing the side wall but looking over your shoulder (along dotted line) to determine the type and direction of service. Once the ball has been struck, move forward (along arrowed line) to cut it off on volley if possible.

point of view. After all, if your opponent has learned how to serve the lob service and rarely makes a mistake, you must quickly learn how to retaliate.

As the receiver, you are under pressure from the server, whose prime objective is to make things as difficult as possible for you. He is under no pressure and has the initiative, which you have to try and gain from him by placing the ball as far away from him as possible. After serving he will have moved to the one position which dominates the court – the T. From that point the furthest place on the court is one of the corners.

The first thing to learn is where to stand so that you have the best chance to return service adequately. In diagram 8, you will see that you should stand in the back corner near the centre line. From there you can look sideways towards the server and determine the type of service with which he will be presenting you. As soon as he has struck the ball, you can anticipate where it is going and if possible cut it off on the volley before it lands along the back wall or in the corner. Move from your receiver's position in a line towards the nearest corner of the service box.

The ball has to land in the receiving quarter, and working on the principle that it is easier to move forwards rather than backwards, you should not stand anywhere other than position A to receive. From there you can quickly move forward to any part of the receiver's quarter.

The safest return of service is a straight drive parallel to the side wall in your quarter, hit to a good length. This can be either a drive after the ball has bounced or, preferably, a volley. Equally successful is a lob, driven or volleyed, along the side wall to a similar length. Both these shots land in the back corner and force your opponent to move from the T towards the back of the court, leaving the T position vacant for you.

Variation is obviously desirable in returning service. However, it is vital that you master the safe returns before attempting more advanced and sophisticated shots. The other safe return is a cross-court lob into the far corner. To be successful this shot must have plenty of height and should be kept as wide of the T (and therefore as near to the side wall) and as deep as possible. In both cases this is to avoid your opponent. These are the two principal safe returns and remember, 'when in doubt, play safe'.

If you decide that your opponent's serve is not formidable, as soon as you have determined the ball's direction there are three basic offensive strokes you can employ to give you the initiative. The straight drop shot to the front corner nearest to you and the crosscourt drop shot to the far front corner are both difficult shots to play with accuracy, but may provide you with the means to move your opponent up the court while you gain the T position. Both

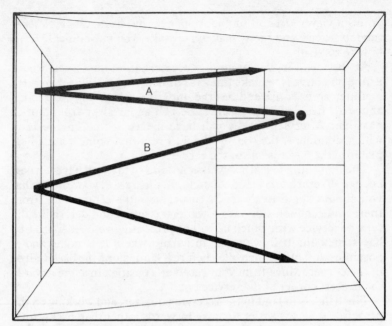

Diagram 9a Safe returns of service: (A) straight drive or lob (B) crosscourt lob.

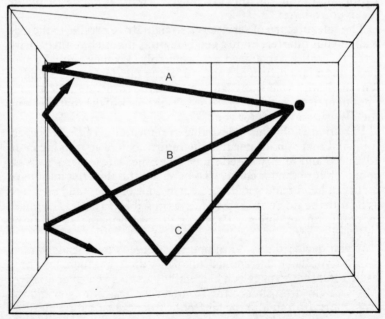

Diagram 9b Offensive returns of service: (A) straight drop shot (B) crosscourt drop shot (C) reverse angle.

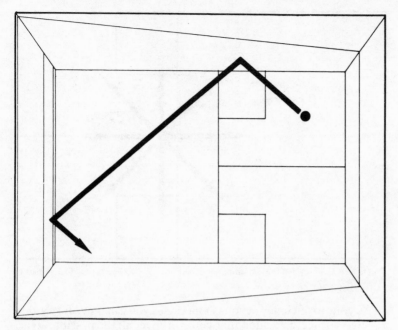

Diagram 9c Defensive return of service: boasted shot.

shots need much practice. They can be played either on the volley or after the ball has bounced.

The third attacking stroke from this position is the reverse angle boast. You hit the ball first on to the far side wall from where it will rebound on to the front wall above the tin and drop back on your side of the court quite far up in the front corner. The service off which you hit this shot will need to have bounced away from your side wall to enable you to get the racket behind the ball.

If a service is very good, then almost certainly the only means of return will be defensive and the use of the boast will be necessary. The boast is a shot that touches a side wall before reaching the front wall. A good service may prevent you from getting the racket sufficiently behind the ball to hit it straight down the side wall. In this case you will have to aim it at the side wall at such an angle that it will rebound on to the front wall above the tin (preferably close to the far front corner). By using this shot you can turn a difficult situation into an advantageous one by once again forcing your opponent, into one of the corners. See diagram 9c.

The boast return should be hit in the same way as a drive but the racket face should be sufficiently open to carry the ball across the court to a point above the tin; the point of impact should be between the body and the side wall.

37

Diagram 10 Command of the T position: from here you have fast access to all four corners of the court.

As your proficiency at squash increases you can move forward to receive service, provided that you still cover all the possible areas. Standing a yard further in may help you to return services more easily on the volley but it may also force you to step sideways or backwards occasionally to dig out a good service.

If a service glances off the side wall on to the back wall before bouncing and the ball comes out into the centre of the court, always try to back up and return it without turning round and hitting the ball on your other side. This can be dangerous as your opponent will almost certainly be within your line of fire. If you back up towards your opponent without turning round, you have the added advantage of pushing him off the T as he has to move out of your way.

Remember – if a service is difficult to return, play a safe or defensive shot. If it appears to be easy, play an attacking shot, but keep the ball away from the T and the centre of the court.

Now for a look at the basic tactics of squash.

Basic Tactics
With the forehand and backhand straight drives as the bread and butter shots of squash, your first attempts at practising hitting the strokes should be concerned with correct timing. Once you have mastered the timing, everything else will follow, including power. Timing is all important.

This book has so far been written as if every squash player was right-handed. Of course this is not the case but as most players are,

38

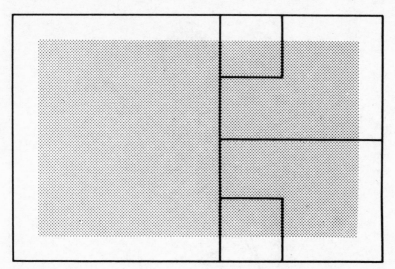

Diagram 11 Ideally, keep the ball out of the shaded area, i.e. the centre of the court.

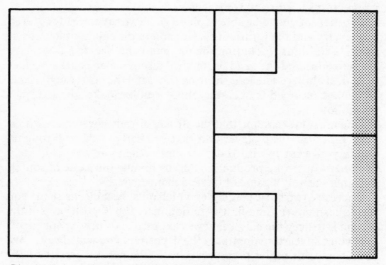

Diagram 12 A good length straight drive should have its second bounce in the shaded area.

Diagram 13 The correct stance at the T – knees bent and racket ready.

I have catered for the majority. I apologise to those left-handers who have read so far and, before going further, would venture to suggest that you have already found it easy by now to interpret the instructions to suit your own game.

In order for you to be able to play a game we have already covered the service and the return of service and in the course of looking at these basic shots (including the forehand and backhand) we have also encountered the need for tactical discipline on court as well as technical ability. The lob, the drop shot, and the boast (angle) have all been mentioned as well and a more detailed look at these strokes will follow.

One must first assume that the strokes already covered are within your repertoire as a player and that you can put the ball roughly where you want it with those strokes. When you are completely proficient in stroke production and technique the game of squash becomes entirely a game of tactical manoeuvre.

There are two basic principles which must become instinctive on the squash court. The first is to dominate the T position and the second is to keep the ball as far away as possible from your opponent.

If you can learn to dominate the T position you will always have your opponent under pressure. The T (the point where the half-court line meets the short line) is the one position from which you can move fastest to any of the four corners. As soon as you have hit the ball, you should immediately move back to the T to prepare for the next shot from your opponent. Don't stand and enjoy your own stroke, however perfect, as you will lose valuable moments.

You should never let the ball out of your sight; watching your opponent, or better still, his racket, will give you a valuable clue as to the probable direction of his next shot. As soon as the ball is hit, you will be able to react faster if you have already anticipated its direction from watching how your opponent hit it. Be on your toes, and move with the ball after he has played his stroke.

As it is your earnest intention to command the T position, it may also be in your opponent's mind to do the same. If he manages to get there first, it follows that the second most important lesson in tactics is to keep the ball away from your opponent and away from the centre of the court and the T in particular. If you let your opponent get to the T and you don't keep the ball out of his reach, he will send you to all corners of the court making you use up valuable energy. You must not let him gain a position in which he can control the rallies.

Diagram 10 shows how easily your opponent, if he is on the T, can control the entire centre area of the court. One step takes him to within striking distance of the side walls and the areas in which a weak return may land. In order to keep the ball away from him when he is on the T, you must hit shots that do not land in the centre of the court. They must land within two feet of the front, back, and side walls, forcing him to move out of position.

Always hit to a good length if you can. It does not matter how hard the shot is, provided that it lands in the right place – within a short distance of the back wall, preferably in one of the corners. A perfect length for a drive occurs when the ball does not bounce a second time; instead it hits the back wall and drops forward on the floor so that no racket can scoop it up.

When stepping on to the court for a game or match you always start by knocking up and getting the ball warm. You should hit the ball as you would in a game – don't relax just because there are no points to be won. If you usually hit the ball hard, then hit the ball hard. Find the rhythm of your game immediately so that when the match starts you know how to adapt it. Don't waste the knock-up; use it to get into the right frame of mind and to loosen the muscles. Your efforts will immediately give you an advantage and enable you to play the game your way.

Don't allow your opponent all the shots he likes in the knock-up. Just as you are trying to establish your authority, he will want to do the same. So if he likes hard drives and volleys, don't give him any. Let him do his share of the work to keep the knock-up going. Don't actually keep the ball away from him – merely send him the sort of

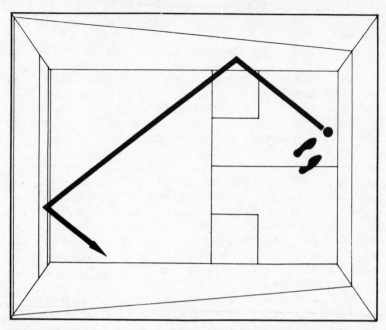

Diagram 14a Taking the ball off the back wall: if there is not much room to manoeuvre, boast the ball off the side wall on to the front wall.

shots you think he would find hard to play so that you have the advantage when the game starts.

Tactics should always be varied from day to day so that nobody can feel that they have a psychological advantage over you because they can anticipate your tactics.

Tactics should never be the same, not only to keep your opponent guessing but also to take account of the speed of the court, the ball, the opposition, and of course, how you feel. Adapt your tactics to suit the conditions.

We have already seen the tactical purpose of the lob service – to hit the ball too close to the side wall for your opponent to volley and too deep in the corner for him to dig it out effectively (if at all). We have also seen the tactical returns of service that can be employed to make your opponent move from the T. Shots to the back corners will draw him away, and shots to the front will help him expend energy provided they are close enough to the side walls and do not bounce out into the centre of the court.

In discussing tactics and the T position, this is also perhaps the moment to mention the correct stance while at the T. Standing straight up with your racket trailing will not help you if you have to make a fast move. Therefore bend your knees, keep your wrist

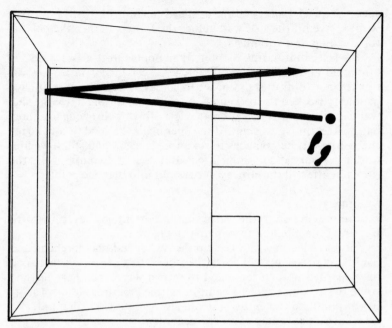

Diagram 14b Taking the ball off the back wall: try to hit the ball straight to the near back corner off the front wall.

cocked with your racket head up, and remember that it is easier to move faster when you are on your toes, slightly stooping to give yourself extra 'leap' potential.

The need to command the T position is now firmly in your mind and you are aware that correct positioning on the court will result in your having to cover surprisingly short distances (compared to an opponent who never succeeds in reaching the T).

When taking the ball off the back wall, you should either face the back wall or the side wall. Give yourself room to hit the ball – don't stand too close to the spot where you expect it to bounce. It may come off the back wall direct from the front wall, or indirectly via a side wall. Only a ball that is a perfect length need beat you.

If the ball lands close to the back wall and does not allow much room to manoeuvre you will have to hit it sideways and upwards, boasting if off the side on to the front wall. However, if you are restricted to the back of the court like this, try and hit the ball straight to the near back corner off the front wall (see diagram 14b).

In moving to the T position, be careful not to get in the way of your opponent if he is attempting to return the ball from behind you. If he hits you with a ball which would otherwise have gone straight to the front wall the point is his – and you are probably very sore. A squash ball travelling at speed can hurt like hell! If the ball would have hit the side wall before the front wall then the point is replayed – but it still hurts.

One last point in this chapter. If an opportunity arises and your opponent gives you a shot off which you can hit a winner, go for it but try not to muff it. In order to achieve that position you have probably worked the ball and your opponent up and down the side walls until an opening was created (possibly by throwing in a short ball to keep him guessing). If the opening looks good to you, go for the winner. If he manages to scramble it back, you still have him under pressure and nothing is lost. But don't miss it or put it in the tin – not after all the effort you have put into that one point.

Summary
Before moving on to the remaining important strokes, it is worth pausing for a moment to sum up this chapter.

You have learned how to grip the racket and play forehand and backhand drives up and down the side walls and across court. You have learned how to serve and to return serve. You have learned some basic tactics and the value of simple practice. Here is a short list of points to remember – if you always bear them in mind, you may have an advantage over the next man.

1 Always watch the ball – even on to your opponent's racket. (Don't stare at the front wall waiting for his shot.)
2 For perfect stroke production, remember the importance of correct positioning of the feet.
3 Prepare early for your shots. Hold the racket cocked at all times so that the backswing is both easier and quicker.
4 Don't stand and admire your elegant drive, but prepare for the next one.
5 Get to the T and keep control of it.
6 Keep the ball away from the centre of the court and your opponent.
7 Vary the play. Always keep your opponent guessing.
8 Adopt the correct stance at the T, bending the knees and holding the racket ready. You are then ready to pounce on your opponent's stray shots.

Become proficient in these basic principles and you will have a foundation on which to build and develop a sound game.

3 FURTHER STROKES

The Lob

We have looked at the basic strokes and must now look at slightly more advanced, but nonetheless essential, strokes in any squash player's armoury.

When you enter a squash court and hit the ball for the first time, it is natural to hit it from below, bringing the racket from behind in an upward path. This, in its most elementary form, is the basis of the lob, which can be used as an attacking shot to win points or as a defensive shot to get out of a difficult position or to give yourself breathing space. The versatility of this shot makes it important.

The ideal lob will land in almost exactly the same place as the lob service – i.e. it will come off the side wall on its falling trajectory and will bounce before hitting the back wall close to the corner. The difference between the two shots is that the lob service must be hit from the service box, whereas the lob can and should be used from anywhere in the court. Thus, the ideal lob is one which is hit crosscourt to make use of the side wall to slow its pace before dying away right at the back of the court.

To play this shot the ball should be struck from below up towards the front wall, so that it rebounds further upwards and travels in an arc to fall as vertically as possible. Unless you are positioned close to the front wall, the ball should hit the front wall about or above the cut line but at least four feet below the boundary line. If you hit above that area you will find the ball will either go out (hitting the ceiling or roof) or have insufficient power behind it to carry it to the back of the court.

However, power and pace are not necessary elements of the lob. The most important factor is accuracy, as you only need to hit the ball firmly enough and at the right angle for it to rebound off the front wall to the back of the court.

The basic stroke for the lob is therefore the same as for a drive on either side, but the backswing should be substantial and the ball should be struck at a point in front of the front foot. The racket head may be allowed to drop below the wrist for this shot if necessary. The footwork is the same as for other shots, with the front foot forward; but the racket face should be open to lift the ball on its upward path to the front wall, and the ball should be hit from below. Hit the ball firmly – a mis-hit lob will either be volleyed fiercely if it is short, or it will come out into the court where it can be dealt with more easily if it is too deep. If you choose to hit the ball late, you will need plenty of wrist action to scoop it up.

In spite of being unspectacular, the lob is a most effective way of breaking up an opponent's rhythm and can give you great satisfaction – particularly if your opponent is so beaten by it that he can

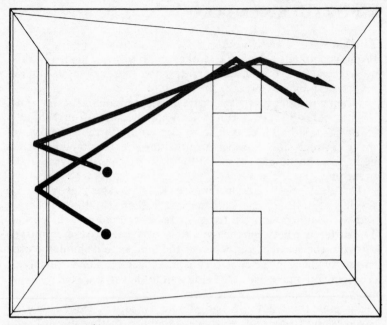

Diagram 15 Lob from front of court: ideally this should be crosscourt. A straight lob must be of a good length and avoid the side wall above the out of court line.

only stand and watch without any attempt at a return.

The object of the lob is to hoist the ball over your opponent so that, with luck, a weak return will be produced. Meanwhile you can take over the T position he has had to leave. The crosscourt lob is most effective as it makes use of the side wall to slow it down. The straight lob, while staying close to the side wall, must also be of a good length but can be more easily volleyed as the margin for error is even smaller than the crosscourt shot. The boundary line on the side wall must be avoided which usually means the ball must fly nearer the T position.

Be careful before you start lobbing that you have mentally taken in the height of the ceiling or the lights. It is no use hitting an otherwise perfect lob if you find that on that particular court the lights hang down and your lob hits one. All courts vary in height.

As the lob can be used so effectively for both attack and defence, you should practise it from all parts of the court. It can be hit from either side after the bounce or even on the volley. It is also possible and often necessary to play a boasted lob – i.e. a lob that hits first the side wall and then the front wall before rising over your opponent to the back of the court. Remember a good lob is always a safe shot. Whether played offensively or defensively, it can always become an

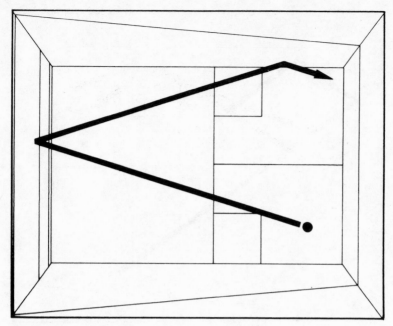

Diagram 16 Lob from back of court: crosscourt backhand.

attacking shot by virtue of moving your opponent from the T into the back corners.

The Volley

The volley is the stroke that cuts off the ball in the air before it has a chance to bounce. When you consider how much the ball is in the air and how frequently it is possible to hit it before it touches the ground, you will realise how important the shot can be.

The volley is basically an attacking shot – with it you are able to dominate the game by not allowing your opponent sufficient time to recover. The volley is also an alternative means of returning the ball to the drive or any other shot from further back in the court. Rather than let the ball travel to the back of the court and possibly create problems, because you then have fewer means of return at your disposal, you cut if off by taking it early. This does not allow your opponent any chance to dominate the front of the court.

Keep the racket head up, as the time available for backswing may be limited. The volley is a short punch with a reduced backswing and a short follow-through. The basic shot is similar to the ordinary forehand and backhand strokes with the point of impact level with the front foot for the straight volley, though this can be

47

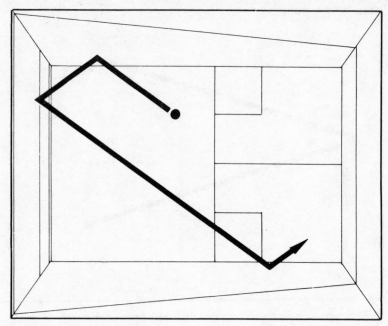

Diagram 17 Boasted lob: after hitting the front wall, the ball rises over your opponent and lands at the back of the court.

varied according to the direction you wish the ball to take. The volley action, on either forehand or backhand, is a movement of the wrist and arm – you do not need to put your whole body into it. It is more of a quick reflex action than any other stroke in the game.

The volley can be used in any part of the court to great advantage, e.g. the return of service, but it is most effective as an attacking shot when you are positioned in the forecourt. Striking the volley from this position will produce many winners for you if you aim just above the tin and, preferably, close to the side wall so that the ball dies away in the nick.

The volley needs a lot of practice. Many players find the forehand volley easy but make mistakes with the backhand volley above shoulder level. It is entirely a question of practice, timing, and correct positioning as well as strength in the forearm and wrist.

The volley is a key shot in top squash – the more you can volley, the more you can dictate the pace of the game and save yourself a great deal of running, as well as putting your opponent under constant pressure. To hit volleys correctly from in front of the short line you should go forward as you hit the ball, having the backswing already in position (with the wrist cocked) and keeping your eye on the ball. Maintain your balance on the front foot (if necessary use your other hand to balance the body). Aim to strike

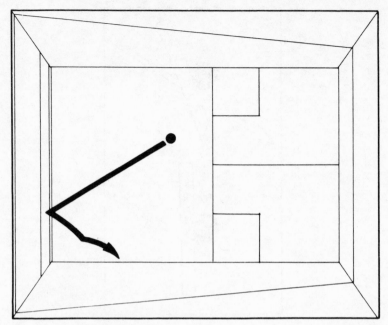

Diagram 18 The use of the cut volley will reduce the distance between bounces so that the ball will 'die' more quickly.

the ball in mid-air at a point that is neither too ambitious to reach nor too low for you to be able to place your racket behind the ball. The shot can be hit with a slightly open racket face to reduce pace, or straight with a closed face to kill the ball.

The use of cut on the volley can be usefully employed as it will bring the ball down from the front wall at a more severe angle and will shorten the distance between the first and second bounce. However, before learning how to cut the ball on the volley or any other stroke, learn the basic shots and be proficient in their use. The cut is executed by using an open racket face and by bringing it down and across the ball to impart underspin. (See diagram 19.) Slice may also be used on the volley – with the same motion, but holding the racket face vertical and parallel with the front wall. The effect is similar. If you find yourself on the wrong foot faced with a volley, play safe; either hit it high across the court or up and down the side wall using an open racket face for control.

If you are at the back of the court, all the same principles apply except that you should treat the volley as a drive struck before rather than after bouncing on the floor.

The Smash
The smash is also a version of the volley and is used to prevent an

Diagram 19 (A) Use of cut on the volley (B) use of slice on the volley.

opponent's lobs landing deep in the court. In order to smash correctly and safely it is necessary to maintain an open stance so that you have flexibility of direction – in other words, when you reach up and can still aim for either front corner. The weight should be on the front foot and you should bend your back to give the shot extra whip, as you may have only a short backswing. Hit the ball well in front of you, down and towards one of the front corners, and follow through fully but carefully avoiding your opponent.

The Drop Shot
The drop shot can be played on either flank like all the other principal strokes, but produces more winners and more mistakes than any other. The drop shot is a winner if executed correctly; if not, the ball will either be set up for your opponent or in the tin.

The drop shot should nearly always be played from the front of the court i.e. in front of the short line. Greater accuracy is possible the nearer you are to the front wall, but the principal reason is to avoid your opponent. You should only consider a drop shot if your opponent is behind you, for if he is in front, it would be senseless to give him a ball which is nearer him than you. There is one exception to this – it is often possible to play an effective drop shot from the

Diagram 20 Forehand drop shot. At this stage you are still in a position to deceive your opponent, i.e. you could play a drop shot, or a drive to either side of the court.

back of the court down the side wall. Don't attempt to hit a crosscourt drop shot from behind your opponent until you have convinced yourself in practice that you can not only do it but that it will be winner.

The action for the drop shot should begin with a full backswing to deceive your opponent into expecting a drive, a lob, or any other shot for which the backswing is the same i.e. except for volley or serve. You must bend your knees and get down to the ball which should be struck at the height of its bounce – with the racket parallel to the floor and the wrist cocked. You must strike the ball firmly but softly (or else it will come out too far into the court) from behind and slightly below. The racket face should be open and the ball should hit the front wall only an inch or two above the tin before rebounding towards the side wall. The perfect drop shot is the ball that rebounds from the front wall into the nick (the join between the side wall and floor).

The positioning of the feet for this shot should be the same as for the drive – the front foot forward etc. – and the ball should be struck just in front of the front foot on to which the weight of the body should have been transferred at the moment of impact. The body should be well balanced to enable you to strike firmly but softly through the ball with a short follow-through.

51

Diagram 21 The perfect drop shot from the front of the court – into the nick.

The shoulder should point towards the corner into which you are aiming the ball. If the ball does not go into the nick, it is better that it hits the side wall before bouncing on the floor. This will slow it down and keep it further away from your opponent.

The best time to go for a drop shot winner is when you are at the T and your opponent is behind you, having made a return that has come out into the centre of the court. Your drop shot should be towards the corner furthest away from him so that he has to travel the longest distance and expend energy in doing so. In addition it moves him right up the court, leaving it open for you.

The drop shot is sometimes used after you have run fast to reach the ball, tempting you to hit it hard. However, anticipate this and move with calculated strides towards the ball so that your balance is perfect at the point of impact. This will help you maintain control of the ball.

Thus, the drop shot can be played straight to the nearest side wall (diagram 21) or crosscourt (diagram 22). You hope that both will land in the nick. The drop can also be played as a stop-volley (e.g. on return of service) which is a block shot, holding the racket out and giving the ball a short downward jab so that it loses pace. The drop can be sliced or top-spun depending on the circumstances and on your confidence.

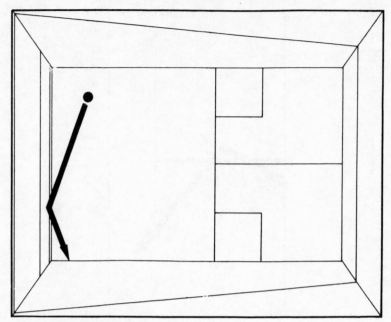

Diagram 22 Forehand crosscourt shot.

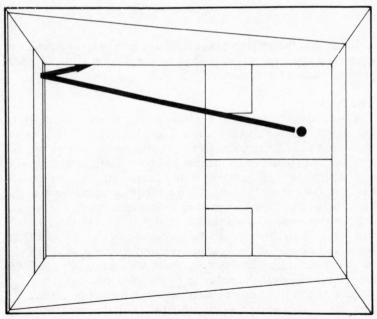

Diagram 23 Drop shot from back of court: can be volleyed as a service return.

53

Diagram 24 The nick: when the ball lands at the join of floor and side wall, failing to bounce – it 'dies'.

Tactically, the drop shot is a useful weapon to use occasionally to keep your opponent guessing and vary the rhythm of play. It often produces a point or two.

The Nick
The expression 'the nick' is used when the ball comes off the front wall at an angle towards the side wall and lands in the join between the side wall and the floor. If it is a perfect nick the ball will fail completely to bounce and the shot will be an outright winner.

The nick shot can be played from a ground stroke (after the ball has bounced) or on the volley, from the front of the court or the back. Whatever happens, an attempt at hitting the nick if you are in a position to do so is worthwhile; if it fails as a nick shot, the ball will rebound off the side wall but stay close to it and lose pace from contact. The nick is the best possible way to end a rally. A well-executed and successful nick is a most satisfactory shot and will boost your morale while reducing your opponent's.

Control and timing and choice of occasion must be perfect. As you play, you should be well balanced and well prepared with your racket at the ready position. From the front of the court, be sure

54

Diagram 25 The nick shot from the back of the court.

you can play the shot you want – you will probably need a week return from your opponent so that you are sufficiently well-positioned to go for the nick.

If you decide to go for the nick from the front of the court, do so when your opponent is behind you and deep in the court as if your timing is slightly wrong this will be a difficult shot for him to reach. Start the backswing early, and keep it short. Keeping your eye on the ball, your weight should come forward on to the front leg and you should strike the ball with an open racket face in front of the front leg and follow through briefly. The knees should be bent. The action in this part of the court is similar to the technique for the drop shot – of which the nick is the most important type.

The nick can also be played with great effect from the back of the court although here there is a far smaller margin for error. The ball should be struck as for a drive, but not hit fully with normal driving pace. The crosscourt drive that lands in the nick is one of the finest shots in the game, but it is also one of the hardest to execute correctly. Hours of practice must be put in before you can ever play it with regularity – let alone under pressure from an opponent in a match.

4 ANGLES

During the course of previous chapters the subject of angled shots (or boasts, as they are known) has cropped up several times in explaining the fundamental points of stroke technique and the use of the various strokes. A boast or angle is a shot that is hit indirectly to the front wall; in other words, it is a return that strikes one or more of the other three walls first before hitting the front wall.

Angles deserve a chapter to themselves; not only can they not be considered elementary, but also a full understanding of angled shots and practical expertise in their use can convert an ordinary player into a mature tactician.

The use of the angled shot is one way to take advantage of the squash court's four walls. Whereas the basic drives up and down the court are the strokes on which your game is founded, the angled shot is more sophisticated and can bring infinitely more variety into play. The squash court is a specific size (21 feet wide and 32 feet deep) and you should learn to use every inch of it to move your opponent around and place the ball in positions which are as awkward as possible.

Apart from using the angled shot for this purpose, it can also extricate you from difficult situations. Very often, a shot hit to the back of the court is impossible to drive because you cannot move your racket round it to put enough power into the shot. The answer is to boast the ball off the side wall on to the front wall. This is a defensive measure and can be done in two ways.

For a drop shot or nick, you aim for the ball to come off the side wall and travel across the court to hit the front wall in the far front corner; or you can skid-boast the ball, hitting upwards and forwards against the side wall, with the ball then hitting the front wall above the cut line fairly close to the centre and flying on upwards to glance off the other side wall and down into the back of the court. After the ball has hit the first side wall, it should travel a path similar to that of a lob service or crosscourt lob.

It is an ideal shot to play when you are stuck at the back of the court with your opponent on the T, being forced to play defensively. The value of the angle shot is that it can be played offensively or defensively, depending on where you are in the court, and can also be used to turn a defensive position into an attacking one.

In striking the ball, the technique is the same as for a drive with the weight on the front foot at the moment of impact, a good backswing, and ample follow-through. The ball needs pace as it has to contend with the deceleration which impact with the side wall will cause. There is only one way to learn how to get the angles right and what amounts of lift you will need to carry the ball – and that is to go on the court and experiment until you are satisfied.

Then practise what you have learned by trial and error until you can play the shot with regularity when you need it.

The angle shot can be played on either the forehand, the backhand, or even as a smash. It can be played from the front or the back of the court. It is particularly useful when your opponent is behind you as, if you shape up to it correctly, he can easily be deceived about the ball's direction. He may anticipate a drive down the wall, a drop shot, or even a lob. He may also anticipate an angle shot but if you hear him coming you can change it. For instance, if you are in the front of the court and he anticipates (in spite of your deceptive stance and backswing) that an angle shot is to be played against the forehand side wall, bringing the ball over across the court to the backhand side wall, and he moves in that direction, you can instantly change your plan and hit the ball early down the side wall leaving him stranded. See diagram 28a.

To hit a forehand angle shot is not technically different from the other shots, i.e. backswing, good balance, wrist cocked and racket up, weight on to the front foot and knees bent, racket face slightly open, eye on the ball maintaining the wrist cocked, and follow through after hitting the ball. The moment of impact will depend on the direction you wish the ball to follow and the extent of holding the racket face open will depend on how high you need or intend to hit the ball on to the side and front walls. If you hit the ball too early you will naturally end up with a cross-court shot, and if you hit it too late your ball may not reach the front wall. See diagram 29.

These angle shots are all straight angles – i.e. a straight angle shot is hit towards your nearside side wall. The reverse angle shot is hit towards the far side wall. See diagram 27a. The reverse angle is useful as a deceptive shot – you can make the motions of playing a crosscourt drive, then instead of hitting the ball opposite the front foot you can hit it early so it hits the far side wall first and moves along the front of the court, hitting the wall and landing back in your side. Your opponent, if he has misread your shot and been duly deceived, will be left groping just behind and to the back of the T, to which position he had moved in anticipation of your drive.

These are some of the uses of the angled shot. Basically, use the angle as an offensive shot from the front of the court and a defensive shot from the back. Use the extra time these shots give you to regain position and balance.

We cannot proceed without a quick mention of the back wall boast. This is not a shot to be encouraged unless you are in severe difficulty, because it is so easy to set up an opening for your opponent. If the ball has passed you completely in the back of the court and will not be rebounding from the back wall as it is such a good length, you can turn to chase it and hit it upwards against the

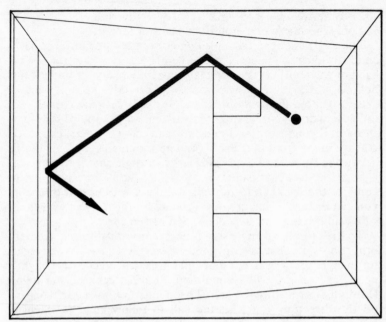

Diagram 26a Simple forehand boast.

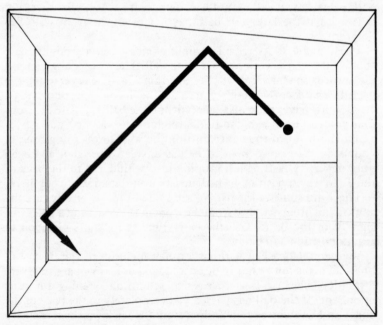

Diagram 26b Boasted crosscourt drop shot.

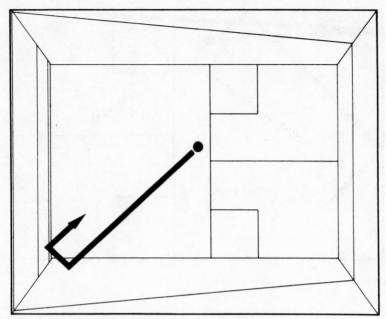

Diagram 27a   Reverse angle shot: hit towards far side wall.

Diagram 27b   Skid boast.

Diagram 28a (A) Use of angle instead of (B) drive from front court.

Diagram 28b (A) Use of angle instead of (B) drive from back of court.

Diagram 29 Intended boasts – errors: (A) the ball has been hit too early, hence a crosscourt shot (B) too late, hence the ball hardly reaches the front wall.

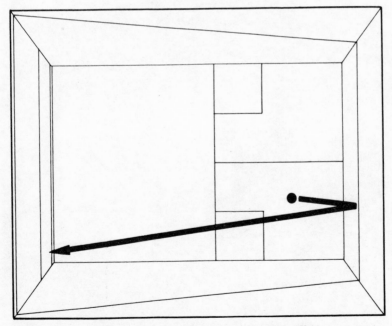

Diagram 30 Back wall boast: to be used only as a last resort, as it is difficult not to set up an opening for your opponent.

back wall with sufficient pace to carry it over to the front wall. The pace at which you strike the ball is not as important as the angle. Hit the ball in a direction as parallel as possible to the side wall; if it hits the side wall and has not been struck with sufficient pace, it may not reach the front wall. The best place to aim for the ball to hit the front wall is certainly in one of the corners. If it lands in the middle it will be an easy return for your opponent. Use this shot sparingly – when it is the only course of action.

5 ADVANCED TACTICS AND PRACTICE

Advanced Tactics

There are so many different ways in which a squash player can hit the ball and so many variations of each shot that inevitably there are limitless ways of playing a point or rally. One of the most exciting and enthralling experiences is to watch a match between two high-class squash players each looking for and trying to capitalise on the other's weakness. If there is no obvious weakness, the struggle becomes almost intellectual as the ball weaves a design about the court that makes full use of the space available.

If and when you have mastered the various stroke techniques and are able to hit the ball more or less in the right direction (i.e the direction in which you are aiming) then the game becomes a battle of wits between you and your opponent, assuming that he is of a similar standard. The wits required will be tactical wits, and the outcome of the match will probably depend on the tactical ingenuity of one of the players. This presumes, of course, equal standard not only of stroke production, but also as far as fitness and stamina are concerned.

Basically, the art of tactics is placing the ball where your opponent will find it hardest to reach and making things as difficult as possible for him (strictly within the rules and a normal code of conduct). Your winning tactics should start before you go on court. This is not to encourage the use of strong-arm tactics in the changing room – 'the last chap I played here was taken off to hospital with blood oozing from more than one wound' type of thing. That is definitely nothing to do with squash tactics and is to be discouraged, apart from the fact that your opponent may decide to despatch you in a similar fashion.

Tactics start with your equipment. You need clean white clothes, a properly strung racket, and shoes without broken laces. Then you must think of the background of the match, i.e. is it an individual or a team event. If it is a team event, which member of the opposing team will you be playing; have you played him before; who won – and why – and how; what are his strong points. What is his forehand like, and his backhand. If you have not played him yourself, possibly one of your team-mates has. The more you can discover about your opponent before you start, the better equipped you will be in your mind about how to deal with him. That is match preparation which must form part of your overall strategy.

When you arrive at a club for a match, especially if the club is unknown to you, check the courts – the height of the ceiling or roof – to see if you can use your lofted lobs. Is it a fast court (hot) or a slow court (cold)? These conditions may have an effect on the way you want to play the match.

Diagram 31 Mistake area: the shaded part of the diagram shows the area where more then 50% of point-losing errors are made.

Tactics have been mentioned all through this book, as an early guide as to how to start moving the ball around the court, and in connection with the individual strokes. This chapter is to try to help you string together the purpose of tactics as a whole, by relating the individual tactics which can be utilised for each stroke. In a way every stroke played is like a brick in a wall; when one brick is laid, you have to lay another until you get one layer which amounts to a point. The layers are added on until you have a wall nine layers deep – the nine points your need to win a game when you have built three perfect walls, then you will have won the match.

The point of looking at it this way is to see the importance of each brick in the wall, or each stroke in the rally. Do not think of each shot as it comes along – think ahead and work out how best to manoeuvre your opponent into a losing position by building up a series of strokes that will move him up and down and across the court. His energy reserves will be used up, which can only benefit you in the long run. If you move him around enough, he will eventually make a slip and either hit a ball that you can play for a winner, or make a forced error himself. Each shot should be a tactical part of the whole strategy you are planning to win that point.

Concentration will be required to keep the plan going and also to notice any weakness in his game. You cannot afford to let your mind wander, and you do not have time to stand and watch your shots or your opponent's. You must keep the pressure on him all the time – try not give him time to think or plan.

Any plan you do devise must, of course, be flexible. Your opponent will certainly have different ideas about you gaining the upper hand and will his best to keep *you* under pressure. Thus, you cannot plan more than a few strokes ahead as he will probably try to put you off your plan by introducing a devious shot or two of his own into the fray. This may put a temporary spanner in the works, but you must not allow it to deter you from subtly returning to the original plan or devising a new one. While working out your strategy, don't allow yourself to neglect your opponent's strong points, and the way in which he has played certain points or shots up until the moment in question. If he seldom missed the nick when given a high forehand shot along the side wall, then the chances are that he will not miss again and you should keep the ball away from that area.

When you start a match, use the knock-up to see if your opponent has any obvious, or even hidden, weaknesses. Also use it to accustom yourself to the court and the pace of the ball. From then on, do not stereotype your game – keep experimenting and changing so that your opponent does not become used to a particular pattern of play. Mix your serves, giving him a majority of lob serves but throwing in a hard service or two for good measure. However, if he is finding your lob service easy to read and is coping with it too well for your liking, you should change it quickly and then come back to it later when it is hoped that he will be out of the habit of hitting winners off it. Change can be accomplished by altering the height, the pace, or even the direction of the service.

When the game is in progress, remember the principal points – try and dominate the T position and keep the ball away from your opponent, then bring your expertise with lob, drop shot, boast, and volley into play. Go for safe shots unless a winner seems certain and keep the pressure on your opponent. Play away from him and keep him behind you as much as possible.

The art of deception should also be used in sending your opponent in the wrong direction. The backswing, footwork, and timing are vital ingredients of any stroke, and taking these items a stage further you should learn to deceive your opponent into thinking you are aiming for one shot and then playing another, e.g. shaping up for a forehand drive, then hitting the ball late and using a boast instead. Deception should be used to get an opponent moving in the wrong direction to create openings.

Gamesmanship and Tactics
Gamesmanship can be considered to be a form of tactics in most games. It appears in squash as in other games – particularly in needle matches that mean a great deal to both winner and loser. Gamesmanship is not, perhaps, the most gentle form of tactics but it can be used to good effect – if you are in need of that sort of assistance. Personally, I feel that there are two types, one of which may be used and the other which should be avoided.

The aim of gamesmanship at its most effective level is to disturb your opponent's concentration and, usually, to make him annoyed.

Personally I do not like its use in this form. An opponent who tries to annoy me or upset my concentration is not the sort of opponent I will play more than once, unless forced to do so.

It is fair enough to capitalise on an opponent's condition but this cannot really be termed gamesmanship. If an opponent is out of breath, and you don't wait for him to recover, that is still fair play. By all means, keep him under pressure like that.

Equally, it is fair to play upon an opponent's weakness, such as a poor backhand volley. But you must decide whether to concentrate your efforts on hitting the ball continuously towards his backhand (in which case it may improve) hoping he will send back a weak return; or whether you should only concentrate on his weak shot when you really need to put the pressure on and gain a point.

In the same 'fair' category must come the question of age. If your opponent is older than average for an active squash player, it stands to reason that although he may have years of guile and cunning that he can use to good effect on court, he is also less agile and his legs will not last as long as they used to. Move him around, make him stretch, bend, and run, for these are legitimate means of tiring your opponent and gaining the upper hand.

Gamesmanship is not cheating, although sometimes it is so close to it that the distinction is almost imperceptible. Remember one thing – very few, if any, champions have had recourse to the art of gamesmanship to help them win. They have been far too concerned with vital aspects of their own progress to stoop to methods that might be considered dubious.

Practice

Squash has an immediately obvious advantage over nearly all other games because you can practise alone for as long as you wish. All you need is a court. It may not be so enjoyable to practise like this, but there is no doubt that it is the only way to really improve and perfect your strokes and your ability to vary their use to fit the occasion. The maxim 'practice makes perfect' may be a bit corny but it still holds true. Practice can also provide you with plenty of exercise if you are sufficiently self-disciplined not to be lazy about it.

Most people practise too little and play too much, though others find practice as invigorating and enjoyable as playing. The main object is to improve, but the exercise value will also do you good.

When practising, be sure that the strokes you are playing are the correct ones – it is just as easy to learn faulty technique on a stroke as good technique. Groove the shots rhythmically until they become automatic. We have looked at all the strokes in the book – now it is for you to practise them – first alone, and then with a partner.

Ball control must be high on the list of priorities for practice.

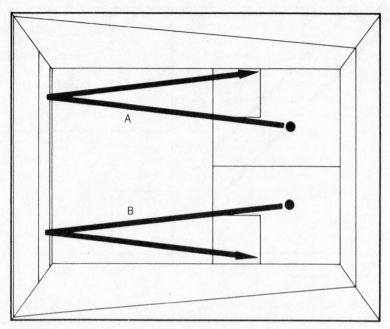

Diagram 32 Practising (A) forehand drives and (B) backhand drives: stand just behind the service box and hit the ball up and down the side wall.

Diagram 33 Ball control: stand at A and hit the ball so that it bounces between the dotted line and the short line, then try drives to the back of the court, i.e. into shaded area.

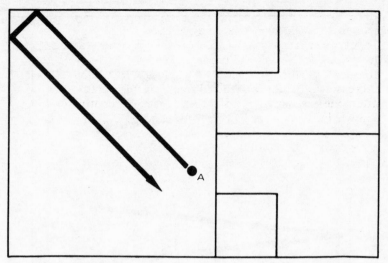

Diagram 34 Angles: stand at A and play the ball to the side wall by the forehand corner so that it returns to you. Repeat.

Until you can control the ball, you will be lost. Irrespective of where you are and how the ball is hit to you, can you hit it in the manner and direction that you have chosen? You need good reflexes to move into the correct position to hit the ball at all, apart from hitting it in the right direction. To do this well you must learn ball control by constant practice.

Learn to use the entire size of the court in terms of moving your opponent around; place the ball where he is not, or where he will find it hard to reach – either by a direct shot, or by a deceptive shot which will make him change direction. Ball control is needed for these manoeuvres – control before power or pace should be your maxim.

A lucky shot is something you cannot practise. Desperate lunges at the ball may result in occasional points, but do not rely on them to win matches for you. Don't bother to practise the blocked service return hit off the wood. If you do it in a match be thankful you were lucky enough to hit a return at all and practise the real thing afterwards.

Control, timing, flexibility in changing the shot after you have begun the backwing, change of pace – all these points should be practised in conjunction with the shots. Practice conditions should be similar to those for a match and your mental discipline must force you to work hard at it. Only if you have experienced real pain in terms of hard work in practice sessions can you hope to have the stamina and graft to outlast a tough opponent on court.

Each shot should be attempted from a new position with variations of pace and spin – and of course you must work at these shots from both the forehand and the backhand sides.

Several short practice sessions are thought to be better than a few long ones. It appears that between sessions, provided that they are frequent, the mental processes are able to absorb knowledge which increases the ability on court after the interval. In other words, after one session has finished the mind will continue to absorb knowledge from it, so that there may be a marked improvement in performance between one session and the next, as long as the interval is not too long.

Individual Practice

Practice on your own is obviously harder work but in the long term it will certainly be worth it. To begin with, use the practice sessions to groove your strokes and gain experience while also introducing the possibilities already mentioned, such as change of pace, spin, and height.

The first stroke to practise is the drive. Place yourself in the forehand court just behind the service box and hit the ball up and down the side wall. Each shot should land in the service box. Practise until you get 10 out of 10 shots in the box. This will help you acquire the instinctive ability to hit the ball to a reasonable length.

Next, practise the same thing with the backhand drive. Don't worry too much about the pace until you have found the length; then increase the pace. Divide the drive into sections – before, during, and after, and go through the technique for each section carefully, applying it studiously to the practice sessions. The drive into the service box cannot be practised too often.

As an additional ball control measure, move forward to the T and practise hitting the ball so that it lands about three feet from the front wall. Imagine a line parallel to the short line a yard up the court and hit the ball back to yourself somewhere between the imaginary line and the short line. This is merely useful for ball control as you are close enough to the front wall for a shot hit with pace to make you react fast to return the ball satisfactorily to the front. Your reflexes and ball control can be improved by gradually speeding up the process until you can carry out this exercise at a fast pace five or six times consecutively.

Then move your practice to the side walls at the back of the court. Stand about four feet in front the back wall and practise your drives up and down the side wall. Try to hit to a perfect length as much as possible and try to keep the ball up and down the side wall. When you begin to find it really difficult to return the ball, you are making good progress – for in other words you are beginning to beat yourself.

Diagram 35 Drop shot: start 4ft from the front wall and work slowly back until you reach the T.

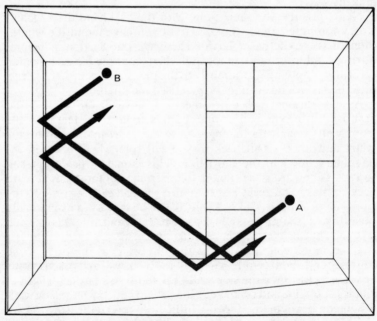

Diagram 36 Practising in twos: A hits a boast from the back of the court, while B returns with a crosscourt drive to the side wall.

In practising the drive you can also practise hitting the ball from the same position early, at the top of the bounce, and late – but in the same direction, i.e. not using the early position to bring the ball round as in a crosscourt forehand. This will help you develop the use of the wrist in determining the direction of the shot.

Moving on from the drive, practice sessions should always include serving. The service is the only shot in the match for which you have time to prepare. It is probably less interesting practice, being less active than the other shots, but it is still most important.

Don't go on practising until you are bored. If you do, the benefit of the session may be lost. Only continue for as long as you find it enjoyable and interesting.

Individual practice can include angle shots, volleys, and drop shots. For angle shots you should position yourself to the left and slightly in front of the T. (As in diagram 34.) Play the ball to the side wall by the forehand corner and it should come back to you so that you can continue to practise the same stroke.

With volleys, stand about six feet from the front wall and hit the ball to and fro without letting it touch the floor. Gradually increase the distance from the front wall and try to keep the ball going in the air.

The drop shot can be practised quite far up in the front of the court. Start four feet away and work slowly backwards until you are practising from the T (diagram 35). All these variations will give you the ability to repeat the shots you need in a match, after much practice.

Practice with Partner

Practising with a partner you can repeat many of the exercises which you set yourself as an individual. However, as those exercises are probably better practised on your own, use the time you have with a friend to do something more constructive.

The most useful form of practice in twos is to have one player in the front of the court on one side and one player at the back on the other. With this formation you can practise the lob, the boast, the drop, the volley, the crosscourt drive, and so on. As you have a partner you can keep pressing him as if he was an opponent, trying to beat him although each of you is only allowed to use one basic stroke. This creates the right atmosphere and will assist both of you to concentrate harder (diagram 36).

To repeat – the most important thing to practise in order to improve is hitting the ball to a good length. Unless you are able to do this, you are unlikely to go very far.

71

6 COURT BEHAVIOUR AND SAFETY

It is important to realise at an early stage that both you and your opponent are moving around at speed in a fairly confined area. Your opponent will often be very close to you and sometimes too close for safety, whether he is in front of you where you can see him, or behind you where you cannot. You must learn to limit your swing in such a way that the racket does not become a dangerous weapon.

You and your opponent must ensure that you give each other room to play and that you do not hinder each other's right to return the ball. Be particularly careful with the follow-through which has been known to cause severe injury. It is not necessary when you are at close quarters for your racket to continue its follow-through at the same pace after the ball has been struck. This should diminish in pace and you should attempt to keep your racket closer to your body and under control. In spite of the small area in which squash is played, it is quite easy to play safely and still enjoy the game just as much. Don't allow your, or your opponent's, enjoyment of the game to deteriorate because of dangerous play.

You should always arrive a few minutes early for a match or even a friendly club game. This is not always possible, but you should always intend to leave a few minutes spare between arrival at the club and going on court to play. You may need to park the car, or your bus or train may be delayed. Too many club players tend to arrive at exactly the moment they are due on court. They have rushed to get there, have to pay the court fee before playing, and to change, and consequently arrive on court five minutes late. Not only is this bad manners to your opponent but you have also missed valuable court time. Quite apart from that, you will already be out of breath and flustered while your opponent will have his eye in and his mind on the game.

If you are playing in a match, you are allowed five minutes for a knock-up. Use the time to have a proper one, and accustom yourself to the feel of the court and the ball. Allow your opponent an equal number of balls to hit. There is nothing more annoying than having a knock-up with someone who never seems to send you any. Offer to change sides when your opponent feels he has had enough of one side.

When the time comes to open the match, if you are serving make sure that your opponent is ready to receive. Do not begin until you have looked over and seen that he is in position.

Once the match has started, the important thing is to keep out of your opponent's way. The correct tactical approach is to head for the T position at the first opportunity, but that is not much use if your opponent is already stationed there. Do be reasonable about your right to the T position. There is no reason why he should give it up if you have been unable to manoeuvre him away. Likewise, if you are dominating it, don't move if you can legitimately keep your opponent at bay.

If your opponent asks for a let, give it to him – it is better not to argue. You may feel that he doesn't deserve one, but if he is able to ask then he must feel that he does. If you feel he was wrong, try not to let him have any more by keeping out of his way. Also, if you hit your opponent with either racket or ball, apologise properly and offer him a let if the occasion justifies it or if you yourself would expect a let in similar circumstances.

Another important point to consider in terms of court manners is when you are obstructing your opponent, albeit by mistake, from taking a shot at the ball. Don't wait for him to ask for a let; give it to him automatically if you know it is your fault.

If you are in front of your opponent at any time and the ball is his to return, then if he hits you it is his point if the ball would have gone straight to the front wall. Therefore it is obviously better (and more comfortable) to keep out of the way.

If there is doubt about whether a ball was up or not, it is always better to play a let unless you have a marker who can make the decision for you. Never knowingly take a point for a ball that has bounced twice or that you have hit twice.

One last point. If you wear glasses and you are taking up squash, you may like to consider the advantages of contact lenses. It is perfectly possible to play squash wearing glasses but unless you are extremely careful they may slip and be broken. Also, if you happen to be playing a rather wild opponent, there is a chance that in his enthusiasm his racket may dislodge your glasses and possibly cause injury. Not only may you feel less vulnerable wearing contact lenses, but some people claim that vision is improved more with them than with glasses.

7 FITNESS AND TRAINING

Fitness
Squash requires a good eye, a strong wrist, great activity, and considerable judgement for success. However, the most important thing in squash today is fitness in terms of stamina, strength, and speed. Of all modern popular sports, squash has the highest rate of energy expenditure.

Fitness for squash consists of increasing the efficiency of the heart, the muscle cells, the circulatory system, the lungs, and so on. As far as the heart is concerned, fitness will require an increase in the heart muscles' size; with muscle cells, the volume of muscle must increase; with the circulation, the blood will need to move move faster in greater quantities to the right areas; the lungs will need increased capacity, and the body will need to be rid of excess fat. All these organic improvements can be achieved by taking regular hard exercise which will result in an all-round improvement of body efficiency, including more stable heat dispersion. Heat loss can be a problem if you are unfit, resulting in a too-fast rise in temperature, which can be dangerous. If you are fit, heat dispersion is more regulated, taking a more even course.

Fitness also means that agility, coordination, reflexes, and balance are all at their peak. The degree of physical fitness depends on general health and nutrition. One cannot be physically fit without a balanced diet of proteins, fats, carbohydrates, minerals, and vitamins. In other words, eat plent of meat, fish, eggs, fresh vegetables, salads, cheese etc.

Moderation in both food and drink is recommended. Alcohol should not be consumed in large quantities – it is genuinely harmful to the system, however enjoyable it may be at the time. There is certainly nothing wrong or harmful about the consumption of wine or beer, but not before playing. In fact, if you are competing in a match it is suggested that you decline offers of alcohol for the previous 24 hours or so. Never play on a full stomach. Be sensible about what you eat within a few hours of playing. There are, of course, exceptions to the rule, but by and large you will find it more comfortable not to eat anything heavy two or three hours before playing.

Smoking has been proved to be positively harmful to health generally. It is also particularly bad for the sportsman who needs all the capacity his lungs can give him and therefore it is generally discouraged.

Fitness refers principally to stamina; the best way to increase yours is by running, which is covered in the training section of this chapter.

74

Speed is another element of fitness. Without it you cannot hope to return to the T fast enough, or to reach the ball if it is hit away from you. Anticipation and quick thinking can save you some energy but unless you are playing somebody who cannot take advantage of your sluggishness (in which case you are very lucky) you will need to develop speed. This is covered in the next section as far as circuit training is concerned. However, there is a test you can do with a friend to develop both your speed and general fitness. Take a box of old squash balls on court (12 balls) and empty them out all over the court. Then time yourself running round and picking them up. Then let your friend do it. Do this two or three times, each time trying to do it faster. When you start again next day or a few days later, try and beat the previous fastest time. This exercise need not, of course, be done on the court.

If you have not played squash before or if you have not taken any exercise for a long time, start gently. Hit the ball around for 15 minutes or so on the first day and gradually build up. It can be disastrous to take violent exercise all at once when you are not used to it. Your heart may not like the sudden extra work it is being made to do, or you may pull a muscle you did not know you had.

Sleep

The amount of sleep required by an individual will vary depending on occupation, age, and possibly sex, although it is not clearly established that men require more sleep than women. Some people require at least eight hours sleep a night while others are able to survive on far less. Some people, too, are able to restore themselves with short naps of a few minutes at a time. If you are used to a certain pattern of sleep then it will be hard to break it – you will find it tiring to change until a new pattern becomes a habit.

Once again, we encounter variations that depend on an individual's way of life or metabolism. If your job entails using your mind, it is generally thought that you will require more sleep than a manual worker. Young people certainly need more sleep than old; in fact, it can be said that as you grow older you require less and less sleep, although the average requirement for an adult is estimated at about eight hours per night – thus one third of your life should be spent asleep in order to get the most out of the remaining two thirds.

Occasional lack of sleep will not have any detrimental effect but regular loss will result in tiredness and lack of concentration. You may also become short-tempered. However, it is unlikely that permanent damage will arise from consistent lack of sleep and the ill-effects it causes, as nature usually intervenes well before such a stage is reached. One really good night's sleep can help you 'catch up' on a considerable deficit.

Sex

A great deal has been written about the effect of sexual intercourse on the sportsman. However, I do not propose to go into detail in this book on the subject of sex and sport. There is nothing to suggest that sex will have a detrimental effect on your squash-playing provided that you have allowed sufficient time after sex for the body to readjust itself. A good night's sleep after sex will be perfectly sufficient to allow your body the readjustment period it needs as well as sufficient sleep in normal circumstances.

Naturally, there are exceptions to this rule. Apparently, at least one world record has been broken by an Olympic champion within an hour of making love. If you wish to experiment on your own individual possibilities, it is recommended that you do not do so when you have a particularly hard match on court to follow.

Travel Fatigue

A short note on jet lag may be be appropriate to the transatlantic or long-distance traveller who also plays squash.

The body has its own time clock that works on a 24-hour cycle, tuned to familiar rhythms at home. When the pattern of living changes by being transported to another continent, the body system is thrown upside down as it tries to live life to the old system while you are imposing a new system and clock. Adjustments to new environments and timings can take up to about a week.

There is no cure for this. However, it is best to try and attune the body slowly to the new system, avoiding an abrupt change. Don't try to play squash within 24 hours of arriving. It may be physically possible, but it may not be sensible.

Training

Circuit training is a succession of carefuly selected and related exercises which are repeated. By courtesy of the BP International Tennis Fellowship, we include here an excellent training programme designed to raise the level of general health and fitness.

Training Programme

This is designed to raise your level of *general* fitness in terms of speed, strength, and stamina. Each week there are three days of running plus exercises, three of exercises only, and one day of rest.

RUNNING

Running is basic to any form of fitness because it improves the efficiency of the body's heart/lung and heart/circulation mechanism. There are three types of running:

Middle distance (1-4 miles). Do this at a fast stride and time each run. Push yourself or it will do you no good.

Intervals. Run for the stated time at a fast stride. Rest for the same length of time. Repeat. Don't flag over the last few.

Sprints. Mark out a distance of 25 yards. Jog up to the starting point and cover this distance flat out.

THE EXERCISES

Press-ups. Front support position on toes and palms with hands a shoulder width apart and body straight. Bend arms. Straighten arms. Repeat.

Sit-ups. Lie flat on your back and clasp hands behind neck. Sit up and press forehead towards knees keeping legs straight. Repeat.

Swallows. Lie flat on tummy and clasp hands behind back. Keep legs and arms stright as you push hands down back of legs while raising head, shoulders, and chest off ground. Repeat.

Burpees. Find a bench or seat that you can step on to only with difficulty. Step up and down on bench getting both legs straight while on it. Lead with left foot first going up and down. Change to lead with right foot after doing half number of repetitions.

Double Knee Jumps. Stand lightly on tiptoe. Leap high off the ground while bouncing knees against chest. Repeat as a continuous rebounding movement without a skip in between.

Pull-ups. Overgrasp on a beam. Without pushing off with your feet pull yourself up until your chin is level with the beam. Lower. Repeat.

Skipping. Get yourself a good heavy rope and vary the steps but always aim to land as lightly as possible. Try to work non-stop for the stated time.

NB It is important to go through the full range of movement 8 each time at each exercise.

THE TEST RATE AND THE TRAINING RATE

We all have different builds and different strengths so the number of repetitions you do at each exercise will depend on your individual capacity.

Before starting on the programme establish your own test rate. Do as many repetitions as you can at each of the exercises in one minute – or until you can do no more, whichever is sooner. This is your test rate. Your training rate is half the test rate (round off odd numbers upwards).

A CIRCUIT

Do each exercise once at the training rate. This is one circuit. Repeat and be sure to do the exercises in the same order as before.

General

1 Before you start any form of training – running or exercises – *always* warm up with five minutes jogging in warm clothing.

2 Remember training is not the end in itself. It is designed to help you to play better squash and is never a substitute for practice. However, fitness is something that no opponent can deprive you of and as competition increases only the fittest will survive.

In addition to the training programme above, carefully supervised weight training can be very beneficial to general strength in important areas – legs, shoulders, stomach, wrists, etc. Another excellent way to strengthen the wrist and build up the muscles is to have a squash ball in the pocket and squeeze it constantly.

Obviously, more sophisticated training procedures are available, but commonsense variations of what has been mentioned above are considered to be quite adequate.

There are some people who claim that the best method of training for squash is to play it. There is certainly an element of truth in that – but it may not be the most effective in the long run.

8 MATCH PLAY AND CHAMPIONSHIP SQUASH

Once the technique of hitting strokes correctly has been mastered, squash reverts to being a game, in common with many others, of strategic wit and stamina. Provided that the physical strength is also there, with concentration you will win points. Squash is a fast game, and the need for tactical expertise will be forced upon you by any opponent of a reasonable standard. In order to bring all your tactical experience to bear upon a match, you will need to concentrate hard, not allowing your mind to wander.

Concentration and determination are complementary, and one will be wasted if the other is missing in a player. That would be a gap in any player's match-playing ability, for it is these two characteristics that help a champion on his way to the top.

When you are playing in a match, do not let your eyes or mind wander from the court. Keep your eyes focused on the ball (or your feet if the ball is not in play), and try to ignore interruptions.

There are many factors that help a squash player to become a champion. Real pleasure in actually playing squash must be a contributory factor. Few, if any, champions at any sport reach the top level without enjoying what they are doing. The effect of success makes it even more enjoyable, just as constant failure can have the opposite effect.

To reach the top, few players can afford not to be perfect in terms of technical and tactical expertise. Beginners have everything to learn and advancement will only come if the tuition is good. The basic strokes must be grasped before additional more sophisticated techniques are learnt. Tactics then begin to play a role, and gradually a player's thinking must concentrate more on tactics than on stroke production. Stroke production should be nearly automatic. A champion develops when all these points are second nature to him and this can only come from years of hard slog and practice.

Practice probably consumes most of the time required for improvement. Consistent improvement comes if every practice shot is executed with controlled physical effort and applied thought. You must be completely dedicated and involved.

Attention to detail also plays a vital part. A champion will not only check that all his equipment is perfect – that the tension of his racket stringing is correct and that his racket handle has a fresh comfortable grip – but will also pay attention to minute detail of strokes and tactics. Attention to detail in the quality and quantity of diet also plays a part for champions.

The will to win and determination and drive that go with it make up an important part of the psychological armoury of the complete player. The 'killer instinct' as it is known is important in key matches when the outcome of one point may change the course of a match. Nerves at the moment of truth can ruin an otherwise brilliant player's career.

So now you are ready to play a match. Obviously there are many points to remember which have been mentioned during the course of the book and which we will not repeat now. But do remember to run after every ball – if you don't, how can you hope to win the point? However you scramble it back, your opponent may miss it – always remember there is a chance.

Playing matches is a natural sequel to learning the game. Any sport, apart from the exercise value, is supposed to instil competitiveness in you, which is what match play does.

Squash reflects the true personality of a player, because everything happens so fast that he has to revert to his natural self. If you are casual, it will show in your playing, and similarly if you are determined or aggressive.

Matches are the proving ground of all your endeavours on the squash court, and this chapter is to help you fulfil your ambitions to win matches. If you know that you are playing a match at a certain time on a certain day, take care not to have a large meal on that day until after the match. Have a light lunch and consume enough fuel to keep your engines running at full pitch for the match. Ensure that whatever food you eat on tha day is full of protein and nourishment. If you have had a steak the evening before, then that will be beneficial to your dietary fitness for the match. Also ensure that you get your full quota of sleep the night before a match – too little sleep, however fit you are, may begin to tell towards the end of a long match.

The subject of clothing has been covered in the early part of the book. If you feel brighter and happier when you are dressed in smart and trendy clothes, why not bring that feeling on to the court as well? Wear clean shirts and shorts, for apart from feeling sharper you will be a credit to your club if you dress smartly – and remember that the clothing should be white.

One top-class player who abhors the use of anything other than a completely clean outfit every time he plays is Gogi Alauddin of Pakistan. If an opponent dares to be so rude as to turn up in dirty clothes, Gogi will be furious and all the more encouraged to wipe him off the court. It should be noted that Gogi is a very gentle and unassuming character.

Attention to detail as far as your racket is concerned has also been mentioned. It may be that you are the proud owner of more than one racket, in which case take it with you and ensure it is in as equally good condition as the other. It would be unfortunate if your racket broke and you had to resort to another which was uncomfortable to hold and had poor tension in the frame. It might cost you several points before you become used to the change.

Do not forget your pre-match tactics. Study your future opponent if you have a chance before playing. Do not watch the ball but watch him – and closely. When his pattern of play emerges you can then plot and plan your tactics against him. If you have not had a chance to watch him, when you go on court you must watch the knock-up and the early stages of the match to find out how he plays. Keep an open mind on your opponent at all times. Don't plot too studiously as equally he may have watched you and devised a special pattern of play for the match – it may be quite different from the pattern you have seen. Points to look for are whether he tightens up or becomes nervous on certain points: whether he is a good volleyer; if he can cut off the ball in mid-court; if he presses home his advantages when in a winning position; whether he falters overhead, how tough he is when losing – whether he fights backs desperately; what his weaknesses are, and so on. These are some of the questions to which you must know the answers. Once armed with this knowledge you can plan a bit further ahead.

In preparing yourself for the match, you must impress upon yourself the importance of *efficiency* on court. The only way to be as efficient as you possibly can is to reduce your margin of error to a minimum. Play a simple basic game – do not aim *one* nick above the tin if you do not *always* hit it above the tin. Aim one foot above for safety to reduce the margin of error. Play all the shots at your disposal safely and try to keep them in the four corners of the court. Efficient play is a stable foundation on which to base your game.

Always try to win by playing your own game and imposing it on your opponent, irrespective of your style of play, be it aggressive, dependent on accuracy, or consistency. The chances of winning a match when you have adapted to the style of your opponent may be limited. Always play within your capabilities and do not foolishly try to do more than you are able.

Play against your opponent's game, not his name or reputation. A determined effort against one who enjoys a better reputation than you is more likely to unsettle him. He has everything to lose and a reputation to gain. This is one of the principal reasons established players lose to those who are less well-known; a good effort shakes them and allows an element of doubt to creep into their minds, causing uncertainty in their play.

Successful match-play depends upon finding your strengths and knowing your weaknesses and making the best of your knowledge. If you find you are losing, try to indulge in a little self-recrimination and decide the reasons. If your tactics are wrong, try to change them. If it is simply because your opponent's shots make it impossible for you to carry out the right tactics, then try to appreciate the fact that you will have to improve – there is always room for improvement.

Perhaps a little more pace on your shots, giving your opponent less time, will unbalance him and disturb his rhythm. You can achieve this either by hitting the ball earlier or by hitting it harder. Experience will show you what to do although the basic principle remains the same.

If you are winning, then keep on with the same tactics and perseverance. It is surprising how many apparently 'won' matches are lost by indiscreet changing of winning tactics.

Assuming that you have practised your shots, that they are working well, and that you are fit, then concentration may be the one single factor that separates a good player from a bad one. Concentration varies among individuals and you must work to improve yours if it is something you find difficult. Never let your concentration slip in any circumstances. It can pull you out of the most depressing circumstances.

Remember that your opponent is human too and that he has feelings and reactions the same as yours. If you are in a tight position, don't forget that he may be suffering in the same way. Tension and physical exhaustion can affect him just as much as you. Don't isolate yourself from your opponent – keep fighting in case he is the first to crack.

You are there to win – so don't go out there to be a good loser.

9 MARKING AND REFEREEING

The incredible growth of interest in this country has resulted in many more individuals playing the game at an ever increasing number of clubs. Both individuals and clubs have become interested in competitions, tournaments, and leagues.

All serious competitive squash matches should be controlled by a marker and a referee. A marker quite often handles the game almost completely, and in fact if there is a shortage of officials at a particular event, he may double as referee. The marker calls the score and makes the decisions while the referee, if there is one present, may be needed to adjudicate an appeal from one of the players on a decision made by the marker. Interpretation of the rules is also a referee's job, and the principal reason for his attendance.

The referee may interrupt a match if he thinks that the marker has made a mistake, or if he feels that a player has infringed the rule on fair view of the ball and freedom of stroke. If the referee thinks a player has not made sufficient effort to get out of the way of his opponent, then he can award a point to that opponent. If a player does not allow his opponent to have a fair view of the ball, i.e. if the ball is shielded by a player after it has hit the front wall in such a way as to prevent his opponent from seeing it quickly enough to make a stroke at it; or of he crowds his opponent by standing too close without actually obstructing; or if he prevents the opponent from having the whole front area of the court to aim for, then the referee should allow a let. However, if the referee thinks the player has done one of these three things deliberately rather than negligently, then he should award a penalty point to his opponent.

There is one more instance in which the referee can make a ruling. If a player is prevented by his opponent from making a winning shot, then the referee should award him a point. It will depend on the referee's experience how he estimates whether a winner could be produced from certain situations; for this reason, it is more or less essential that anyone who marks or referees a squash match also plays or has played the game to a reasonable standard so that he understands the sort of situations with which he could be faced in making a decision.

These points are covered fully in the rules of the game at the end of this book. Obviously, if you are marking and-or refereeing a match, you must first have a clear working knowledge of the rules. Marking and refereeing are both important jobs in squash and not without interest. If you are an enthusiast, neither is a difficult task. A working knowledge of the rules is easy to acquire, because if you play, you will already know a good many of them. The Squash Rackets Association organises courses all over the country which

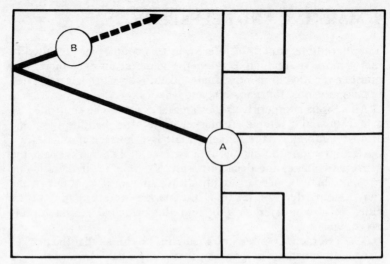

Diagram 37 If the ball hits B before he can return A's shot, then B loses the point.

Diagram 38 If B (intentionally or not) prevents A's shot from hitting the front wall directly, A wins the stroke.

84

Diagram 39 If B (intentionally or not) prevents A's shot from hitting the front wall indirectly, then a let is played.

Diagram 40 If A's shot hit B, but the ball would not have reached the front wall anyway, then A loses the stroke.

are well worth attending if only to learn a bit more about the game.

It will take some time to acquire sufficient knowledge and confidence to mark top-class squash, but small beginnings often lead to other things – and there is a need for markers and referees to assist at competitive events at all- levels. Confidence is needed because you will be required to make quick decisions, instinctively showing that you know what is right or wrong. If you have no confidence in your judgement, your players will certainly have none.

There are many refinements that a marker or referee will need to learn, but it must suffice to simplify the let and penalty situation. If a player is intentionally obstructed he is awarded a point; if it is accidental but he could have hit a winner, he is awarded a point; if it is accidental but the ball could have been returned then a let should be played.

Most of the points a prospective marker or referee needs to know are in the rules. It is not the intention of this book to go into greater detail on the subject. However, a marker should obviously apply common sense to the rules and when he has learnt all the correct calls he can begin to apply his knowledge.

One thing must be remembered. Very rarely have I heard a marker from the back of the gallery state the score sufficiently loudly for all the spectators as well as the players to hear. Quite often only the odd half dozen people close to the marker, apart from the players, can hear it. Everyone there will want to know, so speak loudly and clearly.

As far as scoring is concerned, a squash match consists of the best of five games, each game being won by the first player to win nine points (provided that he is at least 2 points ahead). If the score reaches eight-all, the receiver can decide whether to play *set two* or *no set*. *Set two* means the first player to win the next two points and *no set* means the first player to win the next point – in either case the first player to win the points or point takes the game. In the case of *set two*, the points do not have to be scored consecutively – your opponent may score a point between your two points.

The game does not go beyond 10 points. In the case of *set two*, the score can be 10-9 or 10-8 in favour of one player, and in the case of *no set* the score will be 9-8 to the winner.

10 COACHING

The growth of popularity of squash has resulted in there being too many ordinary players and not enough officials to cope with the expansion. This is not so serious in the case of markers and referees which are part-time jobs, for an occasional evening or possibly a match at a local club. However, coaching is a different matter, for this is not ideally a part-time or amateur occupation. A very reasonable living can be made in this country from it, but in spite of this there is a terrible shortage of qualified professional coaches.

If you want to take squash reasonably seriously, it is often difficult, and in some parts of the country impossible, to find a qualified coach at all. In this case you may have to rely on friends to teach you the basic requirements and hope that they are correct. Unfortunately, it is as easy to become familiar and well-grooved in strokes that are incorrectly produced as it is in the right ones.

Having said that coaching can provide a reasonable living, one should add that it is neither an easy job nor everyone's idea of a profession. Let us just say that it can be worthwhile and interesting. This chapter is for those who may be interested in learning briefly how to start coaching beginners at a club where there may not be another coach. It is possible to attend courses run by the national association and become an Elementary Coach or later an Approved Amateur Coach. This is a highly recommended course of action for anyone interested in coaching though not on a fully professional basis.

It is not necessary to have been or to be a top squash player to become a teaching professional. However, you do need to be proficient and technically correct at all the strokes and at explaining elementary tactics and the rules. In fact, top players are often unsatisfactory at coaching or teaching individuals who have only just started to play because they have forgotten what that stage was like in their own careers, and cannot bridge the gap to an understanding of the pupil's problems.

One notable exception to that rule is Jack Giles, the professional at the RAC, who retired undefeated after being Professional Champion of the United Kingdom for 10 years. When the Lambton Club opened he kindly came and coached some beginners. I was enormously impressed by his communication with his pupils and immediate diagnosis of their problems.

I was equally impressed when in a spare moment I saw him standing alone on the court near the T, hitting the ball to both sides of the front wall in such a way that the ball always returned to him in almost exactly the same spot. He hardly needed to move to keep the ball going – that is ball control.

Thus, communication with the pupil is of vital importance – the ability to get across to him what you want him to learn. Since every pupil is different, the coach must be able to get on easily with all types of people.

When taking a beginner on the court for the first time, you should first introduce him to the various parts of the court. It is not necessary to go into great detail about all the lines and boundaries at this stage but a quick mention of the front wall, the tin, the short line, and the boundary lines should be sufficient to keep him playing in the right direction.

You have probably already helped him choose a suitable racket – not only suitable for a beginner, but also taking into account his economic situation. You should start with a fast ball, as a yellow dot ball will almost certainly be much too dead for him to use. Before actually starting to hit it, you should of course show him the correct grip. Explain why that particular grip is the one to use and why it is successful.

Then place the pupil in the forehand court approximately on the short line and hit the ball to him off the front wall, suggesting that he returns it in a similar way. You may find you have a pupil who has played tennis, badminton, or cricket already, and who knows a bit about ball games and coordination of movement. So much the better. Alternatively, you may find you have somebody who initially seems quite uncoordinated, and who does not respond in the same way at all. In the latter's case, it is a question of perseverance; you must be patient and keep sending him the ball until he finally clicks. You must obviously help as much as you can and try to correct his mistakes – he may not have his eye on the ball or he may be aiming for a ball that bounces higher than the one you are using. Whatever he is finding difficult, you are there to help him.

It is always easier to teach beginners individually so that you can focus your full attention on that one pupil. It may be that you can teach three or four beginners at once if there is a shortage of time or courts, but be careful that you teach them all safety in the court and court manners just as well as you would an individual pupil. Court behaviour is important and should be discussed at an early stage, while safety *must* be discussed at the beginning of the first lesson as soon as your pupil has swung a racket for the first time. Accustom him to the fact that the racket can be used dangerously and cause injury right at the beginning of his squash career, and he will remember it.

Pupils of any age, particularly younger ones, have a limited learning capacity in a concentrated period. Generally, half-hour periods of continuous coaching are quite sufficient. In fact even better would be two periods of 15 minutes each, with a 15-minute gap in between. The increased learning capacity that this introduces is remarkable. However, that is usually impractical.

Concentrated coaching does not mean half an hour of solid talking about how to play. You should divide your time carefully into sections so that a few minutes talking is followed by an equal period of action on the court. If all the instruction is theoretical rather than practical, the pupil will become bored and his mind will wander, defeating the purpose of the lesson. So talk for a short while, then demonstrate, then let the pupil try. Most people learn faster by seeing and doing rather than reading or listening – this applies particularly to squash.

After the elementary start, the first stroke should obviously be the forehand. It should be followed by the backhand and then the other shots in a reasonable order, e.g. service, return of service, lobs, volleys, drop shots, and angles. In teaching all of these strokes be sure to point out the basic footwork necessary, the back swing (safely), the hitting of the ball (correct moment of impact), and the follow-through.

It is important to keep the pupil feeling that he is enjoying learning the game and that he is improving all the time. Don't let him feel uncomfortable at any time – even right at the beginning you must make him feel welcome, that you are personally interested in his progress, and that he has nothing to be self-conscious about. This is all part of the job of communication; the pupil will learn best in a happy and enthusiastic atmosphere.

It may be of interest to some readers that some excellent squash coaching films are available for hire from the Squash Rackets Association, Francis House, Francis Street, London, SW1P 1DE. These are recommended to both coach and pupil.

Part Two

11 THE STATE OF THE GAME

It is estimated that in 1963 there were fewer than 100,000 squash players in the United Kingdom. When this book first appeared in 1974 there were a million and a half players. Now, there are nearly three million regular players and the number is still increasing at an average rate of 2.5 per cent each year, making squash the third largest participant sport in the United Kingdom (behind swimming and badminton). This may not be the same staggering growth rate achieved in the 1970s, but it is still remarkable.

At a time when leisure has become an important business throughout the world, tennis has become a dynamic growth sport in most countries except for the United Kingdom and Australia. In these two countries the number of tennis players has remained fairly static while squash figures have boomed beyond all recognition. It became the fastest-growing participatory sport, particularly in England, during the 1970s, and growth has only recently levelled out. The rate of increase in the United Kingdom has been due to several factors. Public awareness of leisure coupled with a greater desire for fitness has resulted in people taking more exercise. Squash, being one of the most enjoyable methods of escaping from the choking urban rat-race and working off frustrations, was one of the principal activities to benefit. Squash is particularly suitable as a means of physical exercise for executives and those in the professions, and others whose time is important. A game of squash does not take too long and is therefore preferable in terms of time to a game of golf, cricket, or tennis. An added advantage is the fact that squash does not depend on the weather, being an indoor all-the-year-round sport.

In addition, the emergence of a British world champion, Jonah Barrington, captured the imagination of many people. Barrington's attractive personality and particular enthusiasm for the game, and his personal training methods, made him an object of admiration as well as heaping previously unknown publicity on the game.

Another important factor has been the increased provision of local sports centres. Inevitably the authorities have looked for ways of offsetting the losses that swimming-pools incur and have turned to squash courts because of their profitability. These centres have also fulfilled another valuable role in providing opportunities to sample the sport and so ensuring that a feed-in to clubs exists without the prohibitive membership fees being payable until the individual has become keen to play regularly.

Largely due to commercial squash-club developers and promoters, squash began to boom, and the new clubs were quickly
fully patronised. Commercial concerns found squash an attractive
investment because of the substantial income to be obtained from
subscriptions and court fees. With rising property costs, the comparatively small land area required for a successful squash club
makes such a venture a financially profitable concern. And, while
profitable for operators, because of the short time required – in a
half hour one can get a lot of exercise – it is relatively inexpensive
for the regular player.

With more and more courts becoming available (according to
some sources, about 300 new courts are built each year in the
United Kingdom), there has always been the hope that facilities
would go some way towards catching up with demand. In the last
couple of years this has certainly happened in some areas with
waiting lists disappearing and clubs finding it difficult to remain
profitable working on lower ratios of members to courts. In 1974,
with an estimated minimum of one million regular players in the
United Kingdom playing on an estimated 2,500 courts, the average
number of players per court was 400. Now, in 1984, the number of
courts in England alone has increased to approximately 7,800. The
growth rate in the next few years is expected to be in the region of
three per cent.

This appears to illustrate that overall demand is increasing to
such an extent that it will continue to outstrip capacity in the
foreseeable future. However, the experience in some areas where a
temporary saturation point has been reached emphasises the need
for careful management, coupled with more assertive marketing of
individual clubs and recruitment of members as well as continued
national promotion of the sport.

Meanwhile, the interest shown in Great Britain has spread to
Europe. Squash has been played in the United States, Canada,
Australia, New Zealand, South Africa, India, and Pakistan since
before the war, and it has since been taken up by many other
countries all round the world. However, several European countries have only recently become aware of the potential of squash.
Sweden was the first such country to promote the game, and a
boom resulted. Other countries, including France, Germany and
Spain are following suit.

An impression of the development of the sport in Europe can be
gained from a quick look at the statistics of the increases in clubs,
courts and players in some European countries at the end of 1983:

Belgium   80 clubs and 15,000 registered players – an increase
              of 100 per cent compared with the previous season.
Denmark   A doubling of courts from 20 to 40 in one year.

France	180 clubs from 110 at the beginning of 1982.
Germany	500,000 players using 350 complexes comprising 2,700 courts.
Netherlands	Approximately 40,000 players using 400 courts. An increase of 100 courts in two years.
Switzerland	Expansion of 20-25 per cent per annum.

Even the Grand Duchy of Luxembourg has 300 players using seven courts – two of which are restricted to the EEC institutions, one of which has a concrete floor!

In the United States and Canada, a slightly different version of the game is played with a narrower court and a harder, faster ball. In all other countries squash is played according to international (British) standard dimensions regarding size and specification of court, ball, and racket.

There have been several attempts to find common ground between these two different versions of the game. So far efforts to bring the two closer together have been unsuccessful – thus international competition is not yet seriously practicable. However, there is a greater exchange of players across the waters now than ever before. The basic theories governing the two games are similar. However, the international court is two and a half feet wider at 21 feet, the length remains the same at 32 feet, and the board (tin) is two inches higher at 19 inches. Scoring is also different but apart from the court the principal difference between the two games is the ball. The international ball is lighter and squashier, and much slower than the fast, more solid American ball. The racket is the same for both games.

There is an interesting theory behind the differences in court size which is almost certainly true. In 1922, British officials decided to try and standardise the dimensions of the court. Up until that time courts had been built, both in the UK and in the USA, in a bewildering variety of sizes, largely dictated by the amount of space available. An average was taken of some of the lengths and widths of existing courts and the result became the official international dimensions – 32 feet long by 21 feet wide. The same exercise was carried out in the USA two years later, but unfortunately American officials came up with a different answer. The length was the same but the width was only 18½ feet. This difference has really remained one of the stumbling-blocks of a compromise between the two games. It is easy enough to change the type of ball or racket in use, but to alter the size of the court is a very major and highly expensive manoeuvre.

It is in the area of spectator squash that the changes have been most spectacular and offer hope for the sport in the terms of national and international media interest and therefore the positive expansion of all facets of the game. Chronologically the key dates and developments in the last five years read as follows:

September 1978
In Stockholm a prefabricated court supplied by the Swedish Perstorp company was erected in two days in a corner of the centre court of the famous Kungliga Tennishallen (the home of Swedish tennis). This enabled about 600 people, ranged along the banked seating of the tennis auditorium and looking through the glass back wall, to watch the latter stages of the Swedish leg of the World Series of Squash. This was the first of several such enterprises, building a demountable court in a theatrical or leisure hall environment in order to take advantage of larger seating capacities, albeit still only the back-wall.

September 1979
Toronto, Canada was the host for the World Open – at the Etobicoke Olympium Sports Centre in the western suburb of Etobicoke. All 44 integral parts of the demountable court were shipped to Canada and erected in a sports centre with spectator capacity of about 500.

March 1980
The finals of the British Open Championships were played on a Perstorp court erected in the Grand Hall of the Wembley Conference Centre, London. The capacity was 1,200, in great contrast to the 240 seats available in the Wembley Squash Centre next door, home of the Open in previous years.

July 1981
After some promises and false starts, the all-glass court came another step nearer when the world's first transparent squash court side wall was installed. This gave a place in squash history to the village of Walton in Yorkshire. Located at the hamlet, a few miles from Wakefield, is Walton Hall, a hotel, discotheque, fishing and water-ski centre – and a squash club. The side wall of the court adjacent to the entrance was removed and replaced with a Twin-Vue side wall. Twin-Vue is the name of an American company which has developed a system of superimposing tiny black and white dots on the surface of the glass before it is toughened. In terms of the playing characteristics of the court there is no doubt that it satisfactorily meets the non-skidding requirement, by virtue of the roughening effect of the dots.

October 1981
A competitor to the still-awaited all-glass court appeared. It was a plexi-glass court whose proper title was Trans-Wall but it is often

termed 'the plastic court'. The court was produced by a Swedish company, Andren and Sons of Stockholm who used the same dot principle but avoided patent problems by not using glass. All four sides were treated. The court's debut championship was the German Masters played in an air hall in Cologne with viewing on three sides.

November 1981
Glass took another step forward – this time the first glass front wall. For the World Open, held in the Columbus Community Centre in Toronto, a treated front wall was used in conjunction with a plain glass back wall and two demountable solid side walls. This so called 'tunnel court' configuration allowed spectators – and the television cameras – to watch the faces rather than the backsides of the players!

August 1982
A third step in the all-glass story. Twin-Vue unveiled a court with one solid side wall and glass back, front and second side wall in a car warehouse in Milton Keynes, England.

November 1982
The third breed of multi-sided transparent court made its debut at the SRA World Masters event in Leicester. It was the first completely transparent court with viewing from all four sides and was fabricated from 'Perspex', ICI's acrylic sheet. The court has since been used at the British Open culminating in 1984 at the Wembley Conference Centre where the seating capacity was an unprecedented 2,700.

It is these courts which will form the favourable setting for increased and improved television coverage. The greater number of available angles together with the opportunity of covering more closely the players' facial expressions, notably strain, will make television presentation more interesting.

Two more innovations have been tried in an effort to motivate television still further. One is the use of 'American scoring' in an attempt to lessen the attritional nature of rallies. However, while this appears to be effective in the early rallies of each game, as the points tally rises a more defensive posture is adopted. The other development is the use of white balls on transparent courts with floors painted blue and the lines yellow. It is certainly colourful and the optical qualities of white make viewing better for spectators, but the broadcasting difficulties still remained initially. Undoubtedly both innovations will continue to be used and refined in efforts by promoters and governing bodies to make squash attractive to a television audience.

12 A BRIEF HISTORY

The game of squash rackets is generally thought to have had its origin at Harrow School about 150 years ago when boys waiting for their turn to play rackets knocked a soft ball against some walls outside the court.

Squash rackets is really the younger brother of the game rackets, which was first recorded as being played at Harrow in 1820. The dimensions of a rackets court are considerably greater than those of an international standard squash court – the basic overall area is 60 feet by 30 feet, with the back wall 15 feet high and front and side walls about 30 feet high. A modern squash court is 32 feet deep by 21 feet wide with back wall 7 feet high and front wall 15 feet high.

Rackets is played with a hard ball, whereas squash uses a soft ball, with which the name of the game is associated. Originally neither rackets nor squash, with their general similarities, came under the jurisdiction of a ruling body, but in 1907 the Tennis and Rackets Association was formed to administer the games of real tennis, rackets, and squash. It was not until 1929 that the Squash Rackets Association was formed; this body now virtually controls the game.

Whereas real tennis and rackets have remained fairly static in terms of popularity and players, due mainly to shortage of courts – the subsequent higher cost confining these two fine games largely to the older universities and public schools – squash began to develop from the 1930s. Before that time, there was no definitive court size. As late as 1934 it was written in the *Encyclopedia of Sports, Games and Pastimes* that 'the authorities regard a court 42 feet long and 24 feet wide as excellent'. There is no doubt that if a squash court was still to be built to these dimensions the game would not have prospered as much as it has in recent years. However, the dimensions of an international standard squash court were originally laid down by the Tennis and Rackets Association in 1922; these dimensions were confirmed as official when the SRA was formed seven years later.

It is possible to trace the development of the game of squash back to the origins of ball games but it is beyond the scope of this book to offer anything like a complete history of an exercise so ancient and cosmopolitan. It must suffice to give the briefest of histories on the relationship of squash to other ball-and-racket games.

It is known that in the 13th and 14th centuries the game of tennis (real, royal, or court tennis – whichever you prefer) was played in France as a means of recreation and exercise.

Tennis continued to be played throughout the centuries and was truly called the game of kings; Francois I and Henry VIII were two of the many monarchs who used to play. Rackets developed indirectly from tennis as a ball-and-racket game which could be played by one person hitting a ball against a wall. Apart from Harrow, a version of rackets used to be played by the debtors in Fleet prison.

The game of squash soon developed from the earlier versions of rackets and in about 1860 a Major Harry Gem used to play a game at Leamington which historians claim to be the modern origin of the game of lawn tennis. In 1874 a Major Walter Wingfield patented a game called Sphairistike or Lawn Tennis. There is no doubt that this new game took not only its name from the original game of tennis.

The evolution of any game presupposes a past of considerable duration and although the game we know today as squash is comparatively young in its present form, it has a pedigree as long as most modern games.

13 THE ADMINISTRATION OF THE GAME

The Squash Rackets Association

The Squash Rackets Association was formed in 1929 to cater for the needs of a growing sport; up until then a sub-committee of the Tennis and Racquets Association had lent some semblance of organisation since its formation in 1907. Also in 1907 the United States Squash Rackets Association was formed to administer their version of the game.

The SRA is the central authority in England for the game of squash in all matters connected with the organisation and playing of the game with special reference to rules, championships, international matches, disputes, and other such matters. The principal functions of the SRA are to exercise control over the game as well as offering a service to the many affiliated clubs and local authorities with squash facilities. The aspects of control include the rules of the game, sponsorship, public relations, and contact with the Sports Council (often a benefactor in the form of grants).

Clubs can affiliate themselves to the SRA on payment of a fee; in return they can call upon any aspect of the SRA's expanding advisory coaching and technical service. The SRA's experience and expertise in areas of administration, organisation, control and playing of the game are useful to the majority of clubs.

In addition, clubs may participate in leagues and club competitions, hold important matches and tournaments, hold coaching clinics and exhibitions – and enjoy SRA support in organising events, raising sponsorship, and gaining publicity.

As far as the technical service is concerned, this centres mainly on aspects of court construction; design, materials, and so on. Maintenance and repair also come within the SRA's expert knowledge – and its help can even be sought on planning arrangements and the raising of finance for new centres.

The Women's Squash Rackets Association

The WSRA was formed in 1934 to act as the central authority in all matters concerned with women's squash in England, with special reference to rules, disputes, competitions, and team selection. All open tournaments and championships are held under the jurisdiction of the WSRA, which is affiliated to the SRA.

The International Squash Rackets Federation

The ISRF was formed in 1966 to provide an official world amateur championship. This was at the instigation of the Australian Association, who had grown weary of raising the finances to send their best amateurs halfway round the world to compete in the British

Amateur Championships (recognised then as the *de facto* world championships).

Of course, that was not the only reason to form an international body, but there was also a need at that stage to encourage the growth of the game in areas where it did not previously exist. A third object was to have a valid organisation that could settle disputes of an international nature between member nations.

All the world's principal squash-playing nations come under the jurisdiction of the ISRF although many of them have had their own associations for far longer. For instance, Great Britain, USA, Canada, Australia and New Zealand had associations before the war. Egypt and Pakistan formed associations soon after the war and ever since, participating nations have formed their own associations to conduct domestic affairs.

The role of the ISRF has become increasingly more important, and, not surprisingly, more difficult, since the abolition of amateur status in most major squash nations in 1980. Commercial pressures on promoters armed with sponsorship money are a more dominant factor, and the players associations with their interests jockey for position with the governing bodies and other parties.

The European Squash Rackets Federation

Since its formation in 1929 and until 1966, the SRA was acknowledged as the central administrative body for squash throughout the world, apart from the USA. In 1966, the International Federation was formed but continued to use the same offices in London as the SRA. Accordingly, the SRA has been at the forefront of the world development of the international game.

During the past few years the squash boom in Britain has encouraged more interest on the continent and visits to the SRA have become more and more frequent. To foster this increase in potential European development, the European Squash Rackets Federation was formed in April 1973 during the first European Squash Rackets Championships in Edinburgh (to which the SRA invited 10 European nations to send teams).

The Championship was started to stimulate further interest in the game in Europe and the second European Championship was duly held in Sweden in April, 1974. The Championship also provides an excellent opportunity for representatives of national squash interests from the various countries to meet and discuss further development.

The European Federation thus acts as the focal point for the stimulation and development of the game on the continent. At the moment, England and Sweden are able to contribute more in terms of experience but eventually each nation will be able to make contributions of interests to all member countries.

The International Squash Players Association

The ISPA came into being in 1973. Its main object was to promote the game to the best advantage for its members, yet at the same time to be closely involved with the governing body, and indeed all amateur governing bodies.

Its objective over the next five years was to provide continuous competition throughout the year so that a player may arrange his own personal calendar to suit his individual temperament. At the same time, because the sport is extremely demanding, it is expected that most individuals will take a break from the competitive circuit to restore their energy and rekindle incentive and motivation.

Ken Hiscoe became the President of ISPA when it was formed, with Jonah Barrington as Chairman. Since then a number of players have taken on various responsibilities as officers of the Association. They include Hiddy Jahan and Ahmed Safwat. Indeed the level of ISPA activity increased so substantially that in 1982 a full time Managing Director was appointed. His role has been to arrange and administer an integrated circuit which will further the financial aspirations of players and promoters alike. The short-term aspirations of financial rewards for the players balanced with the need for long term development can only be put across with great difficulty to the top current players (who tend to be short-sighted in terms of career development). But it is essential to the growth of the game at the top level that the ISPA management succeed.

Part Three

THE PLAYERS

Hashim Khan

Hashim Khan is acknowledged as the greatest squash player ever. His record of 45 major tournament victories which include seven British Open Championships is testimony to this fact. Perhaps more significant is the indelible impression left with those who saw him at full flight – the impression of unchallengeable mastery.

Still coaching and competing in the USA, Hashim Khan is a legend in his own time, and what is even more astonishing is the fact that he did not compete outside the Indian sub-continent until he was 35!

Hashim also returns to England each spring to participate in the British Open Vintage (over-55) event. Since his first return in 1977 he has an unbroken string of six titles (up to 1983, so far) which may soon constitute a record to compare with his British Open feats.

Born in 1916 at Nawakilla, a village near Peshawar in the North-West Frontier Province of what was then India, Hashim Khan is a Pathan. However, his tribe had come down from the wild Khyber Pass to settle on the plains, and Hashim's father was Chief Steward at the Officers' Club in the British Army's cantonment in Peshawar. There it was that eight-year-old Hashim became a ball-boy for the officers when they hit the ball out of their court, which had no ceiling. Hashim also learned to play by moonlight.

When Hashim was 11, his father died, and from this time his ambition turned to professional squash. He soon gave up schooling to practise by himself for long hours on the squash court. He outgrew the ball-boy service, but waited until he was 28 before being able to take up professional squash coaching. He was appointed coach to the British Air Force in Peshawar.

Hashim Khan first received recognition as a champion when he defeated Abdul Bari in the final of the All-of-India championships held in Bombay. Bari, a cousin, hailed from the village of Nawakilla, but the two had not seen each other since childhood. Hashim's first of three triumphs in this event over Bari was in 1944. It was the former's first match on a court with timbered floors and he was playing before a large gallery, also a new experience. In spite of weighing only eight stone, Hashim quickly returned Bari's renowned drop shots and repeatedly caught him flat-footed.

Only the sub-continent partition and independence problems could halt Hashim's dominance of this event. In 1949, at a time when he was coach to the Royal Pakistani Air Force, he won the inaugural Pakistan Professional Championship from the 21-year-old Roshan Khan, a distant relation, who was destined to follow Hashim to British Open eminence.

When Bari declined an invitation to play for Pakistan, the High Commissioner enquired for another squash player to bring honour to the young nation. The diplomatic corps and the Air Force hierarchy knew little of Hashim's talents, and it was by a close call that he was asked to represent the country in the British Open Championships against the formidable world leader Mahmoud-el-Karim. Karim, the Egyptian professional, was deemed to be the perfect squash player by virtue of his elegant stroking and decade of unbeaten matches.

Hashim Khan, however, demolished the seemingly invincible Karim with sheer weight of shot and pace of foot. The squat, barrel-chested, spindly-legged Hashim ran the tall, languid Egyptian (at 30, five years his junior) ragged. On his return to Pakistan he was heaped with accolades, and even the schools were closed for a day! In 1951 he defeated Karim again in the British Open; later in the same year he went on a tour of Australia and New Zealand.

Hashim's style of play was originally based on the speed with which he could return an opponent's stroke and the accuracy of that return. Usually his shots were low and hard, forcing errors from his opponents. But his eye for the ball left none of his opponents in any doubt that he needed any great range of shots, he could have acquired them. Indeed in successive years when he returned to Britain to win the Open, he improved his stroke-making by displaying a powerful and uncannily severe nick-shot played across the court. His ball control was such that whereas for other players a low, hard drive barely above the tin was an attacking shot, to him it was merely another 'safe' one.

He won with commensurate ease wherever he went, presiding over the squash world until the vagaries of age caught up with the heavy demands exacted by the international style of squash. It was logical that Hashim then turned his hand to the North American style of the game with less emphasis on fitness, plus a greater financial return for his immense skills.

Hashim Khan not only dominated the world during his international playing years, but led, and influenced, the complete national hegemony that Pakistan experienced in global squash competition through their other champions, Azam, Roshan, Mohibullah, and latterly Sharif in North America.

Younger brother Azam, a tennis coach, was persuaded by Hashim to pursue squash, and with close association and training, succeeded Hashim to win four British Open Championships, Roshan Khan from the same 'stable' joined them and Mohibullah Khan, a nephew of all three, became the last of the Khans to take the British Open title, in 1962. As Hashim moved to Detroit, so followed his eldest son Sharif, as did Mohibullah, to set about establishing a new dynasty in the USA.

Hashim Khan has carved a legend in record books around the world as a squash player without peer, and as leader of a nation that ruled the squash world for over a decade.

Jonah Barrington

Jonah Barrington has been the most influential personality in European squash since he burst into the headlines in 1966 by being crowned both British Amateur and Open Champion in the same season.

The impetus given to the growth of squash by the media stemmed largely from the endeavours of Barrington and the style in which he carried them out. In short, he was news. At a time when British world champions were becoming increasingly difficult to find, Barrington sustained his winning form to take every major championship in the world with the exception of the World Amateur. Barrington annexed the British Open no less than six times, and stands only two victories short of Geoff Hunt's record of eight triumphs.

Barrington developed his tremendous tenacity during his childhood in Cornwall, trying to overcome the natural advantage that an older brother holds in competitive play, and in life in general.

Schooling at Cheltenham did little to make the young Jonah feel at peace with the world. His time spent at Trinity College, Dublin, proved to be thoroughly enjoyable from a self-indulgent point of view, but soon it was quite clear that the aimless Barrington was in need of some salvation. This he found in squash; it put meaning into his life, giving him new purpose and a code of behaviour.

Nazrullah and Azam Khan, two remarkable Pakistani professionals, were instrumental in this process. They gave Barrington the inspiration and guidance to tear through the ranks of squash players who stood between him and his goal – to be the best in the world.

To gain the attention of the squash kingdom and the Press, Barrington had to knock the reigning world champion, Abou Taleb of Egypt, from his perch, and subdue the redoubtable amateur, Aftab Jawaid of Pakistan. Once installed at the top, Jonah then had to prove time and again, before hundreds of different galleries, that he was truly the ruling monarch. He had globe-trotted as an amateur, but on tour with Taleb, Sharif Khan, Rainer Ratinac of Australia, and Jawaid, playing exhibitions around the world, Barrington notched up further Open titles in Australia, Egypt and Pakistan.

It was not all plain sailing for the champion, however. Every opponent delights in playing his best against a champion, and there were even those who refused to admit the position he held until the late 1970s. They were chiefly the three Australians, Hunt, Hiscoe, and Nancarrow. An edge in fitness often enabled him to overcome Hiscoe, but for a number of years the lanky Nancarrow spelt trouble for Barrington. Both being left-handers, and Nancarrow, as ungainly as his shots were deceptive, created a nightmare for the Cornishman. Two of Barrington's major ambitions were frustrated by Nancarrow – the 1967 World Amateur title, and the 1969 British Open.

The threat posed by him no longer loomed so large since the series staged in 1973-74 around Britain, during which the two contested a professional 15-match tournament. Barrington won by the slightest of margins, but it was enough to put paid to the bogey. The series was an innovation of Barrington's when he first brought Geoff Hunt from Australia to play in a similar contest in 1970.

Hunt, as Barrington's successor to the British Open crown, was the ever-present threat to the latter's world dominance. He won the 1970 series 13-2, but Barrington retained the Open. Whenever the two met on courts favourable to attacking driving, Hunt would be favourite to win the encounter. But if the air was warm and the walls offered little help to power squash, i.e. it was a slow court, then Barrington could lob his way to victory, albeit in matches which consistently lasted more than an hour and a half. This was testimony to the incredible amount of training that was to capture the attention of the Press in Barrington's early reign, the training which today continues to consume large slices of Barrington's life. Famous are the Barrington excursions to Central Africa, to find peace, sun, and altitude training.

Apart from the rigours of physical training, and Barrington's famous pain barriers which he crashed through *en route* to major titles, many hours have been spent labouring away in squash courts in search of the hallmark of the really magnificent player; ball control. Ball control, even after two torrid hours of squash, was what Barrington had to have if he was to defeat Hunt; so that was what he acquired.

Often criticised for not being a natural stroke player but for simply gaining his titles by retrieving powers. Barrington was grossly underestimated. It is true that he did not have a complete range of finishing shots, for example he had difficulty in dealing with short ground strokes, but the accuracy of placement that he showed in pushing the ball into the back of the court, taking it from any speed, and being able to keep it there, has been the downfall of every opponent at some time in his career.

Barrington's tactics of burying his opponents in the corners of the court, forcing errors or weak returns to be killed with a small, deceptive array of short shots, and running him off his feet, were executed with precision. Always challenging for the centre of the court to dominate proceedings, Barrington is content to win in the end, and so is not perturbed if he loses the first game and a half without scoring himself – just as long as his opponent has become weary for the next phase of the game, when Barrington takes over the ascendancy.

Barrington scored some memorable victories over Hunt in this fashion. His economy of swing helped his tactics. Not only did he try not to introduce a margin for error in his short, abrupt swing of the racket, but he also saved the energy which is vital in the fifth set. This factor was crucial to his last British Open triumph over Hunt in 1972 when the Australian stood two points away from the crown, but had been drained of the strength to even stroke the ball correctly. Barrington swept through the last few points from behind to take the championship by the slightest advantage in stamina.

Barrington has trained ever more assiduously in recent years, battling against his age with great success. In 1979 he amazed the squash world by reaching the World Masters final at Wembley before losing to Qamar Zaman. And in 1980 he ran the risk of losing his record of not having been beaten by an Englishman since 1966 when he entered the British Closed Championship. He came perilously close to defeat in his five game semi-final against Philip Kenyon but beat Gawain Briars in four games in the final to take the title.

Operations on both knees robbed Barrington of a large chunk of his 'squash autumn' but he returned in late 1982 with an avowed aim to annex "Over 35" titles – although he was at this stage already in his forties! He won the British Over-35 comfortably enough but in 1983 he lost in the World Open Grand Masters and British Open Over 35 finals, both times to Ahmed Safwat.

Currently, Barrington's immense motivating powers and wonderful eloquence are being put to use by the SRA, who are employing him to mastermind the development of the national under-19 team.

Apart from the impact he has made on the record books of squash, his immeasurable contribution to the popularising of the sport in Britain, and the cause of the professional player rising under his leadership, make him the catalyst of squash development in Britain over the past two decades.

Geoffrey Hunt

Geoff Hunt, the foremost exponent of power squash, was the world's leading player from 1974 until his retirement in 1982 due to back and hip problems. He disputed Barrington's reign as world champion from 1967 until 1973. However, during this period he only once won the British Open, acknowledged as the ultimate championship. But in the ensuing years he took his total number of British Open titles to eight, passing Hashim Khan's record of seven in 1981 when he narrowly beat prodigy Jahangir Khan in a pulsating final. In years to come it is possible that Jahangir may challenge this record but it is difficult to envisage at this stage.

From Melbourne, Australia, Hunt took up squash at the age of 12. His father Vic was an astute judge of squash, and was a pillar of administration in the boom period of Australian squash. He influenced Geoff's style and tactics with what he had learned from Dardir and the Khans. The result, as witnessed in Hunt's style, was unique, although it had the basic trade marks of orthodoxy. There was nothing fanciful or particularly radical in Hunt's style, although he swung the racket up to a third more than normal, and hit the ball in a much flatter trajectory.

His technique was to rain a barrage of stinging drives on his opponent, sweeping him wide to the back of the court, as he himself controlled the game from centre-court. By using his special athletic prowess and lightning eye, he volleyed as much as possible, forcing his opponent to play shot after shot, in quicker and quicker succession. Then, when the opponent was sagging in the back corners, Hunt angled the ball, making him rush forward. Hunt then covered the next shot at top speed because he aimed to hit it to length before his opponent could recover. And so it went on – relentless pressure, with drop shots and powerful nicks to finish off any stray balls. Hunt's speed of eye, mind and foot enabled him to retrieve a multitude of shots which, against anyone else, might have been winners.

Opponents who did not attempt to play their own shots ended up trapped into playing Hunt at his own game – a fatal mistake. The only style of play which on occasion beat him was the kind used by Barrington and Gogi Alauddin on 'slow' courts where they lobbed remorselessly high to Hunt's backhand. This kept the ball out of the danger of being hit into the nick, forced Hunt on to the defensive and prolonged the rallies. By attacking, they hoped to cadge sufficient mistakes to outlast Hunt, provided that they themselves could play error-free squash. But Hunt countered such strategy by becoming fitter, so that he could beat them at their own game. Zatopek-style 400-metre sprinting was a feature of his training, which clearly succeeded in making him the undisputed number one player in the action-packed tournament circuit in the 1970s.

Four times Australian Amateur, thrice World Amateur, and British Amateur Champion, Hunt won innumerable titles both before and after turning professional late in 1971. In addition, in the National Open titles Hunt included four World Open wins in his portfolio.

Off-court Hunt was a quiet, pleasant man. He gave up his scientific interests – he has a BSc in chemistry – for squash. Although none of his family have been able to match his brilliance on the squash court, his brother, sister, and father have all been leading exponents of the sport in both home-state Victoria, and national (Australian) spheres.

The power and speed with which the dynamic Hunt demonstrated his skills was an attractive showcase for the sport, when he was not faced with the negative tactics of some close rivals. Then the match battle tended to become a question of whether the appalling onslaughts of his attacking style could overwhelm the dull constraints of persistent lobbing.

Jahangir Khan

The parents of Jahangir Khan must surely have had an insight into the future of their younger son when they named him. Jahangir means 'emperor of the world' and there is no doubt that the young Pakistani is emperor of the squash world. Although his ancestry cannot be traced back to the 17th century Mogul King who supplied his name, Jahangir's knowledge of his lineage extends as far as his great great grandfather, a rajah in Peshawar. A couple of generations closer was his grandfather who was one of many squash ball-boys working at the open air courts of the British service clubs on the North West frontier.

Then came Jahangir's father Roshan and his cousins, the brothers Hashim and Azam. All were Khans and all won the coveted British Open title in the 1950s and early 1960s. Thus both his forename and family name have great meaning. Especially as, since the reign of his father's generation, the Khan domination of the major titles has only now been reinstituted by Jahangir himself.

Within only four years of his introduction to the sport, at 14, he became Pakistani Junior Champion; an amazing feat when one considers the depth of talent within the small number of players in that country. But the fairytale continued. At the age of 15 Jahangir was included in the Pakistan party participating in the World Amateur Championships in Australia and won the individual title, beating Philip Kenyon in the final. But so lowly was his ranking that he had not been included in the Pakistan team for the team event which followed, so, holding the world crown, he sat on the sidelines.

Prior to the World Amateur his brother Torsam, a world ranked player himself, had persuaded father Roshan that he could aid Jahangir's development if he came to live with him in England. This was agreed and so Jahangir arrived following his success in

Australia. But within a month Torsam had left to take part in the Australian Open, a tour from which he did not return. Tragically he collapsed and died during the championship leaving the younger player without the arranged guiding hand. However, cousin Rehmat Khan offered to take on the role of guardian in England and so Jahangir was soon back in this country training again.

His next major event was the last British Amateur championship in January 1980, an event in which he was probably the hottest favourite for many years. But another cruel blow was dealt when he slipped on Wembley's number one court on the eve of the championship and damaged his back. Since he was living within a couple of hundred yards from the Wembley courts he spent the days of the event wandering around the centre like a lost child.

Soon though, things improved. Only a typically gritty performance by Jonah Barrington stopped him reaching the quarter-final of the British Open and it was evident to all that in the coming 1981-82 season he would be a force to be reckoned with. And so it proved. The New Zealand, Pakistan and Belgian titles fell to him and in April he was in his first British Open final at the age of 17. Not only in the final but close indeed to taking the Open from holder Geoff Hunt, exactly twice his age. Hunt however managed to hold on in his last win against the teenager.

At the time of writing, Jahangir has not been beaten since his defeat in the 1981 British Open final. In November 1981 he beat Hunt to win his first World Open title and subsequently added his first two British Open titles. In the autumn of 1983 Jahangir won another four world titles when he took the World Masters, World Open, World Individual and was part of the Pakistan team which won the World Team Championship.

That he has not been beaten since April 1981 is a phenomenal achievement in itself, but as a teenager his maturity has been a revelation. The death of Torsam could easily have pushed him out of squash entirely but instead it left him with a determination to win the World Open title for his brother. Credit was also given to 'Allah'. He believes that the God of the Islamic faith will determine the future for him, but one cannot very well ignore the very hard work that has taken a lightweight stringy kid whose principal interest was cricket to world squash champion.

Jahangir's capacity for endurance coupled with intelligence only partly explains the squash phenomenon but additional clarity comes from Jonah Barrington's remark that he 'successfully married the shop-window talents of Pakistan squash with Western training methods'.

Qamar Zaman

Born in Quetta on 11 April 1951, Qamar Zaman hails from Peshawar, the Mecca of squash players. Zaman's rise to the top of the professional game was a rapid one. In 1968 he won the Pakistan Junior Championships, and by 1973 he had won the Australian and Pakistan Amateur titles and reached the finals of the British equivalent. This world class potential became indelibly stamped on the squash world when in 1974 he not only finished runner-up in the British Amateur, but also reached the semi-final of the British Open. In the 1974-75 season, the Rolex, North West, Durham and British Open all fell to Zaman. He turned professional in April 1975 at the same time as Mohibullah Khan.

Zaman's game is unorthodox – his blend of the ordinary with the exciting, and the consistency with which he pulls off the 'dodgy' shot, single him out as a player with the all important quality of 'spectator appeal'.

'The court jester of world squash', 'the most naturally gifted player to be produced in the last ten years', and 'the most unorthodox player with the greatest spectator appeal'. These and many other accolades have been heaped on Qamar over the last ten years, since he shot to prominence with his British Open victory in 1975. It was the intolerable burden of these, and the pressure of being at the top of his profession that caused his slight slide down the rankings from the number one spot which he held in 1975, to his present position at number three. In 1977 he won the World Series of Squash and the Pakistan Masters and was runner-up in the World Open and British Open. He still remains the most exciting stroke maker in the game today when he is on form and has never been ranked outside the world's top three in the past ten years. Only Geoff Hunt, in his era, and Jahangir Khan now, stand between Zaman and the world's top spot.

Hiddy Jahan

Hidayat (Hiddy) Jahan has been a great asset to professional squash. In a period of victory based on fitness, the timely intrusion of a daring shot-maker is a welcome relief.

A generous extrovert, Jahan enjoys life in general and squash in particular. Son of a squash professional in Quetta, Pakistan, Jahan sought to improve his game in Lahore, training with Alauddin and Muneer. As Alauddin captured the British Amateur titles, it was Jahan who was his sole serious contender in Europe. With the Australians absent, only Jahan was able to defeat friend Alauddin; this he managed in the Welsh Amateur and West Wycombe events, where Alauddin over-played his defensive tactics and failed to take the opportunities presented to him.

Jahan, a popular player, was held back from reaching the summit in world rankings by his own impetuous nature, which led him into stroking errors when attempting just one too many breath-taking winners. His impetuosity also led him to express his frustration over controversial refereeing decisions, thereby losing the necessary concentration to win evenly-contested matches.

He turned professional after losing to fellow-countryman Mohibullah in the semi-finals of the 1973 British Amateur Championship. It was a memorable match – Jahan played in a masterly fashion, reaching match-ball in the fourth game only to succumb in a full five sets to the relentless retrieving of young Mohibullah, who went on to win the title. Since then Jahan has reversed the decision and settled the score for that season. Throughout the 1974 Open circuit of tournaments he went from strength to strength, establishing himself as the number four player in the world. What was more significant is the style in which he gained the ranking, and the potential talent still untapped which could carry him further up the rankings. And so it did.

Strongly built, Jahan thumps the ball with searing drives, especially across-court from the forehand. His versatility is amazing, both with overhead and ground strokes. One reason for this is his obvious enjoyment in the success, and another, on a more practical level, is the incredible strength he possesses in his right wrist. He can turn a drop shot into a drive with a flick of the wrist, hence adding attack and accuracy to deception – a potent mixture in a player who thrives on success.

Greater success came as Jahan matured mentally and tempered his stroke-play. He is cast in the die of Hiscoe – that of an attacking player – and is thus a squash player who wants to win off his own inventive racket. He has had his set-backs – such as the railway accident which nearly cost him his life in 1967, and certainly his place in the Pakistan team for the World Championships; his allegiance to friend Sajjad Muneer in 1971, whereby he forfeited his position in the team to New Zealand in a political wrangle with internal officialdom; a bout of malaria that caused his withdrawal from the 1972 British Amateur Championship when seeded number two; as well as several crucial defeats at vital stages of his career. In 1969 he found Saleem a stumbling-block. He passed him, but has recently found Zaman and Mohibullah irksome at critical matches in the Pakistan and British Amateur Championships respectively.

More recently Hiddy overcame his stumbling-block of Zaman in the 1976 Pakistan World Masters Tournament, when he beat his Pakistani compatriot 9-1 9-3 9-4 in 20 minutes. Those who witnessed this no-nonsense display of attacking squash said that it was the greatest piece of precision power play they had ever seen.

Despite his continued high world ranking it was only in 1982 that Jahan managed to reach his first British Open final. Many times a quarter- and semi-finalist he at last took a well-deserved final place before losing to Jahangir Khan. In fact his consistency can be measured by his achievement of only once failing to reach the British Open quarter-finals since 1970.

In addition to providing entertainment on the court he has actively promoted the sport and the interests of his fellow players, and has served as Chairman of the International Squash Players Association. He has lived in Surrey with his English wife Sue for some years and recently acquired British citizenship. Having become eligible to represent his adopted country he did so in the 1983 World Team Championship in New Zealand where he led the English team to the final before losing to Pakistan.

Heather McKay

It was said that no one would be able to match Janet Morgan's record of a decade's supremacy in women's squash – for she (now Mrs Shardlow) reigned from 1949 until 1958. But after only two years, a bright young star emerged from Australia to upset all the odds and prove absolutely invincible from the day of her first triumph in the Women's Squash Rackets Association Championship in 1961. And in 1977, Heather McKay, 35, unrivalled as ever retired. Not only was she undefeated for those past 16 years, but the margins by which she defeated every threat to her position were awesome. Winning the WSRA Championship final in about 20 minutes for the loss of only three or four points was about par for the course that Heather McKay set herself.

Her career was one of isolation – so far was she in the lead. Her closest rivals, particular Fran Marshall of England, and Jenny Irving and Marion Jackman (née Hawcroft) both of Australia, were great competitors, but all failed to close the gap to make real inroads into Mrs McKay's security of tenure at the top. On a rare occasion Mrs McKay dropped a single set in a match, but over the span of 16 years the number of these could be counted on one hand.

Heather McKay's motivation was pure and simple. She enjoyed playing squash, and whilst she did, she wanted to do it as well as she possibly could. So it is because she was a perfectionist that she was driven to train as avidly as she did at first, and that drove her to win by the largest margin she could always. Her continued success was one of the truly remarkable athletic feats of our age, and her style, apart from her strength of character and will power, was a key factor in this success.

For much of her life she had lived in either Queenbyan or Canberra, Australia, while competing for New South Wales at inter-Australian events. Her techniques were fashioned from Sydney, revealing a potent forehand, as well as all the basic tactics employed by that school of thought. Her squash was free from eccentricities and frivolous strokes. The emphasis on sound foot-work made possible by fitness and stamina. The footwork aids the shot production and balance, from which comes the power in the driving to the back of the court. Her disciplined use of angles and short shots moved her opponent around the court until finally a space was made and she slammed a drive into it, clearly out of reach of her harassed opponent. By positioning herself in the centre of the court and being ready to strike the ball early, and then powerfully imparting speed to the ball, Mrs McKay built up pressure on her opponents until the barrage caused a loose shot which was severely dealt with – either by a drive into an unguarded sector of the court, or by crisp short angles and drops.

Although she only turned professional late in her career, Heather's life in the past tended to revolve around the squash court. With her husband Brian, a teaching professional, she managed squash courts, and played exhibitions throughout the world. Now, with Brian, she holds exhibitions and coaching clinics (when not running a squash club) in their adopted 'home' city of Toronto, Canada. But squash has not been a totally consuming passion, for Heather McKay was also active on the hockey field, once again wearing her national colours. In addition, since retiring from competitive squash, Heather has twice been the top ranked player in the world at racquetball, a primarily North American bastard racket sport that is probably already on the decline.

British Players
After the decline of the British amateur squash empire in the early 1960s, it was not possible to revive the supremacy, even with Barrington spearheading the nation.

However, at the present time, England is blessed with three men in the world top ten. In addition to **Hiddy Jahan** (now a British citizen), **Gawain Briars** and **Philip Kenyon** are competing at the very top level.

Briars has been described as the most exciting British player to come on the scene since the emergence of Barrington. He turned professional at the age of 21 in 1979 – a year before amateur status was abolished – and accumulated a string of titles including two British Closed titles. Since 1980 he has constantly vied with Philip Kenyon for the English number one spot which he lost at the beginning of 1984 following a defeat at the hands of his rival in a wonderful British Closed final in December 1983. He finally lost in five games after having a match ball in the fourth. He uses his height of 6' 4'' to dominate the court from the T and his range of shots and attacking squash make him an exciting player to watch.

Kenyon is two years older but has substantially mirrored Briars' progress through the junior and into the senior ranks. He won the British junior championship in 1973, 1974 and 1975 and the Drysdale Cup (British Under-19 Open) in 1973 and 1974. Since then he has captured the British Closed twice and has the distinction of having reached the British Open quarter-finals two years in succession. He did this in 1983 by grace of a magnificent win over Gamal Awad which proved to be the match of the championship. One of the highlights of the career of this hard-hitting competitior was being part of the England team (with Jahan and Briars) which reached the final of the World Championship in New Zealand in Autumn 1983. A 3-0 win against Australia in the semi-final was particularly satisfying.

There are a number of players chasing these three in the domestic rankings but only one, **Geoff Williams**, is making a real impression at the moment. He came close to beating Briars in the 1983 British Closed Semi-final, only losing in five games, and the left-hander has comprehensively beaten all those in the list except the top trio. It is evident that they certainly aren't safe with this rapidly-improving player at present.

The English girls are making even more inroads into the world rankings, spearheaded by the Guernsey girls **Lisa Opie** and **Martine Le Moignan**. Opie, now 20, reached the 1983 final of the British Open before losing to Vicki Cardwell of Australia. This followed her world Junior Championship win. Not surprisingly, the bubbly girl who now bases herself in Nottingham has a string of Open and National titles to her name, and her recent attempts to add stamina to her natural athleticism seem certain to reap dividends in the coming seaon.

Martine Le Moignan is very much a contrast in playing terms to Opie, although they both come from Guernsey and have really accompanied each other up the playing rungs. She is a taller and stronger left-hander but one whose concentration and will to win sometimes let her down when she is not totally mentally prepared for an encounter. She is, however, an adventurous stroke player who has registered wins over all her contemporaries including Vicki Cardwell, the current British Open Champion.

The challenge to the 'G' girls looks likely to come from Surrey's **Alison Cumings** who already has one British Closed title to her credit, and 16-year-old **Lucy Soulter** from Gloucester who is undoubtedly the best prospect to be seen on the horizon for many years. In 1983 she was only just beaten in five games in the semi-finals of the World Junior Championship – by a 19-year-old who went on to win the title! Her engaging personality will also be a great asset as interest in the women's game develops.

Part Four

THE RULES

The Rules are published by kind permission of The Squash Rackets Association

The Singles Game
Approved by the International Squash Rackets Federation (ISRF) to be effective from 1 November 1983. (These rules refer to the game of Squash Rackets in respect of the game as played on courts, the specifications for which were first determined by The Squash Rackets Association of Great Britain.)

1 THE GAME, HOW PLAYED The game of Squash Rackets is played between two players with standard rackets, with balls officially approved by the ISRF and in a rectangular court of standard dimensions, enclosed on all four sides.

2 THE SCORE A match shall consist of the best of 3 or 5 games at the option of the promoters of the competition. Each game is 9 points up; that is to say, the player who first wins 9 points wins the game, except that, on the score being called 8 all for the first time, Hand-out may choose, before the next service is delivered, to continue the game to 10, in which case the player who first scores 2 more points, wins the game. Hand-out must in either case clearly indicate his choice to the Marker, if any, and to his opponent.
Note to Referees If Hand-out does not make clear his choice before the next service, the Referee shall stop play and require him to do so.

3 POINTS, HOW SCORED Points can only be scored by Hand-in. When a player fails to serve or to make a good return in accordance with the Rules, the opponent wins the stroke. When Hand-in wins a stroke, he scores a point; when Hand-out wins a stroke, he becomes Hand-in.

4 THE SERVICE
(a) The right to serve first is decided by the spin of a racket. Thereafter the server continues to serve until he loses a stroke, whereupon his opponent becomes the server, and so on throughout the match.
(b) At the beginning of each game and each hand, the server has the choice of either box and shall thereafter alternate for as long as he scores points and remains Hand-in. However, if he serves a fault

113

which is not taken, or a rally ends in a Let, he shall serve again from the same box. If the server serves from the wrong box, there shall be no penalty and the service shall count as if served from the correct box, except that Hand-out may, if he does not attempt to take the service, demand that it be served from the other box.

(c) The ball, before being struck, shall be dropped or thrown in the air and shall not touch the walls or floor; it must be served direct on to the front wall between the cut line and the out of court line, so that on its return, unless volleyed, it falls to the floor within the back quarter of the court opposite to the server's box. Should a player, having dropped or thrown the ball in the air, make no attempt to strike it, it may be dropped or thrown again without penalty. A player with the use of only one arm may utilise his racket to propel the ball into the air before striking it.

(d) A service is good when it is not a fault or does not result in the server serving his hand out in accordance with Rule 4(f). If the server serves one fault, he shall serve again. Hand-out may take a fault, and if he attempts to do so, the service becomes good and the ball continues in play.

Note to Referees The receiver has not attempted to take a fault until he has clearly committed himself to playing the ball.

(e) A service is a fault: (i) if at the time of striking the ball the server fails to have at least one foot in contact with the floor within the service box, and no part of that foot touching the line surrounding the service box (called a foot-fault). (ii) if the ball is served on to or below the cut line. (iii) if the ball first touches the floor on or outside the short or half court lines delimiting the back quarter of the court required in Rule 4(c).

Note to Referees Any combination of faults in one service counts only as one fault.

(f) The server serves his hand out and loses the stroke: (i) if he serves 2 consecutive faults, excluding any that have been taken by Hand-out, when the ensuing rally has ended in a Let. (ii) if the ball touches the walls or floor before being struck, or if he fails to strike the ball, or strikes it more than once. (iii) if the ball is served on to, or below, the board, or out, or against any part of the court before the front wall. (iv) if the ball, before it has bounced twice on the floor or has been struck by the opponent, touches the server or anything he wears or carries.

5 THE PLAY After a good service has been delivered, the players return the ball alternately until one or other fails to make a good return, or the ball otherwise ceases to be in play in accordance with the Rules.

6 GOOD RETURN A return is good if the ball, before it has

bounced twice upon the floor, is returned by the striker on to the front wall above the board, without touching the floor or any part of the striker's body or clothing, provided the ball is not hit twice or out.

Note to Referees It shall not be considered a good return if the ball touches the board before or after it hits the front wall.

7 LET A Let is an undecided stroke, and the service or rally, in respect of which a Let is allowed, shall not count and the server shall serve again from the same box. A Let shall not annul a previous fault.

Note to Referees This last sentence applies only to a second or subsequent service after a fault has not been taken.

8 STROKES, HOW WON A player wins a stroke:
(a) Under Rule 4(f).
(b) If the opponent fails to make a good return of the ball in play.
(c) If the ball in play touches his opponent or anything he wears or carries, except as is otherwise provided by Rules 9, 10 and 13 (a)(i).
(d) If a stroke is awarded by the Referee as provided for in the Rules.

9 HITTING AN OPPONENT WITH THE BALL If an otherwise good return of the ball has been made, but before reaching the front wall it hits the striker's opponent, or his racket, or anything he wears or carries, then:
(a) If the ball would have made a good return, and would have struck the front wall without first touching any other wall, the striker shall win the stroke, except if the striker shall have followed the ball round, and so turned, or shall, without so turning, have allowed the ball to pass behind his body, in either case taking the ball on the forehand in the backhand side of the court or vice versa, a Let shall be allowed.
(b) If the ball would otherwise have made a good return, a Let shall be allowed unless, in the Referee's opinion, a winning stroke has been intercepted, then the striker shall win the stroke.
(c) If the ball would not have made a good return, the striker shall lose the stroke. The ball shall cease to be in play, even if it subsequently goes up.

10 FURTHER ATTEMPTS TO HIT THE BALL If the striker strikes at, and misses the ball, he may make further attempts to return it. If, after being missed, the ball touches his opponent, or his racket, or anything he wears or carries, then:
(a) If the striker would otherwise have made a good return, a Let shall be allowed.
(b) If the striker could not have made a good return, he loses the

stroke. If any such further attempt is successful resulting in a good return being prevented from reaching the front wall by hitting the striker's opponent, or anything he wears or carries, a Let shall be allowed in all circumstances.

11 APPEALS

(a) An appeal may be made against any decision of the Marker, except for (b) (i) below.

(b) (i) no appeal shall be made in respect of the Marker's call of 'Foot-fault' or 'Fault' to the first service. (ii) if the Marker calls 'Foot-fault' or 'Fault' to the second service, the server may appeal, and if the decision is reversed, a Let shall be allowed. (iii) if the Marker allows the second service, Hand-out may appeal either immediately, or at the end of the rally if he has played the ball, and if the decision is reversed, Hand-in becomes Hand-out. (iv) if the Marker does not call 'Foot-fault' or 'Fault' to the first service, Hand-out may appeal that the service was a foot-fault or a fault, provided he makes no attempt to play the ball. If the Marker does not call 'Not up', 'Out', or 'Down' to the first service, Hand-out may appeal, either immediately or at the end of the rally, if he has played the ball. In either case, if the appeal is disallowed, Hand-out shall lose the stroke.

(c) An appeal under Rule 6 shall be made at the end of the rally.

(d) In all cases where a Let is desired, an appeal shall be made to the Referee with the words 'Let, please'. Play shall thereupon cease until the Referee has given his decision.

(e) No appeal may be made after the delivery of a service for anything that occurred before that service was delivered.

12 FAIR VIEW, FREEDOM TO PLAY THE BALL, AND INTERFERENCE

(a) After playing the ball, a player must make every effort to get out of his opponent's way. That is: (i) a player must make every effort to give his opponent a fair view of the ball, so that he may sight it adequately for the purpose of playing it. (ii) a player must make every effort not to interfere with, or crowd, his opponent in the latter's attempt to get to, or play, the ball. (iii) a player must make every effort to allow his opponent, as far as the latter's position permits, freedom to play the ball directly to the front wall, or side walls near the front wall.

(b) If any such form of interference has occurred, and, in the opinion of the Referee the player has not made every effort to avoid causing it, the Referee shall on appeal, or stopping play without waiting for an appeal, award the Stroke to his opponent.

(c) However, if interference has occurred, but in the opinion of the Referee the player has made every effort to avoid causing it, the

116

Referee shall on appeal, or stopping play without waiting for an appeal, award a Let, except that if his opponent is prevented from making a winning return by such interference or by distraction from the player, the Referee shall award the Stroke to the opponent.

(d) When, in the opinion of the Referee, a player refrains from playing the ball, which, if played, would clearly and undoubtedly have won the rally under the terms of Rule 9 (a) or (b), he shall be awarded the Stroke.

(e) If either the striker or non-striker makes unnecessary physical contact with his opponent the Referee may stop play and award a Stroke accordingly.

Note to Referees (i) The practice of impeding an opponent in his efforts to play the ball by crowding or obscuring his view is highly detrimental to the game. Unnecessary physical contact is also detrimental as well as being dangerous. Referees should have no hesitation in enforcing Rule 12 (b) and 12 (e). (ii) The words 'interfere with' in Rule 12 (a) (ii) must be interpreted to include the case of a player having to wait for an excessive swing of his opponent's racket.

13 LET, WHEN ALLOWED Notwithstanding anything contained in these Rules, and provided always that the striker could have made a good return:

(a) A Let may be allowed: (i) if, owing to the position of the striker, his opponent is unable to avoid being touched by the ball before the return is made.

Note to Referees This Rule shall be construed to include the cases of the striker, whose position in front of his opponent makes it impossible for the latter to see the ball, or who shapes as if to play the ball and changes his mind at the last moment, preferring to take the ball off the back wall, the ball in either case hitting his opponent, who is between the striker and the back wall. This is not, however, to be taken as conflicting in any way with the Referee's duties under Rule 12.

(ii) if the ball in play touches any article lying in the court. (iii) if the striker refrains from hitting the ball owing to a reasonable fear of injuring his opponent. (iv) if the striker, in the act of playing the ball, touches his opponent. (v) if the Referee is asked to decide an appeal and is unable to do so. (vi) if a player, in preparing to play or playing his stroke is, in the opinion of the Referee, distracted by an occurrence on or off the court.

(b) A Let shall be allowed: (i) if Hand-out is not ready, and does not attempt to take the service. (ii) if the ball breaks during play. (iii) if an otherwise good return has been made, but the ball goes out of court on its first bounce. (iv) as provided for in Rules 9, 10, 11 (b) (ii) 18 and 19.

(c) No Let shall be allowed when the player has made an attempt to play the ball except as provided for under Rules 10, 13 (a) (iv), 13 (b) (ii) and (iii).

(d) Unless an appeal is made by one of the players, no Let shall be allowed except where these Rules definitely provide for a Let, namely Rules 9 (a) and (b), 10, 12, 13 (b) (ii) and (iii).

14 NEW BALL At any time, when the ball is not in actual play, a new ball may be substituted by mutual consent of the players, or, on appeal by either player, at the discretion of the Referee.

15 KNOCK UP

(a) Immediately preceding the start of play, the Referee shall allow on the court of play a period not exceeding 5 minutes to the 2 players together for the purpose of knocking-up, or in the event of a player electing to knock-up separately, the Referee shall allow the first player a period of 3½ minutes and his opponent 2½ minutes. In the event of a separate knock-up, the choice of knocking-up first shall be decided by the spin of a racket. The Referee shall allow a further period for the players to warm the ball up if the match is being resumed after a considerable delay.

(b) Where a new ball has been substituted under Rules 13 (b) (ii) or 14, the Referee shall allow the ball to be knocked-up to playing condition. Play shall resume on the direction of the Referee, or prior mutual consent of the players.

(c) Between games the ball shall remain on the floor of the court in view and knocking-up shall not be permitted except by mutual consent of the players.

16 PLAY IN A MATCH TO BE CONTINUOUS After the first service is delivered, play shall be continuous so far as is practicable, provided that:

(a) At any time play may be suspended owing to bad light or other circumstances beyond the control of the players, for such period as the Referee shall decide. In the event of play being suspended for the day, the match shall start afresh, unless both players agree to the contrary.

(b) The Referee shall award a game to the opponent of any player who, in his opinion, persists, after due warning, in delaying play in order to recover his strength or wind, or for any other reason.

(c) An interval of one minute shall be permitted between games and of 2 minutes between the fourth and fifth games of a 5 game match. A player may leave the court during such intervals, but shall be ready to resume play at the end of the stated time. When 10 seconds of the interval permitted between games are left, the Marker shall call 'Ten Seconds' to warn the players to be ready to resume play. Should either player fail to do so when required by the Referee, a game may be awarded to his opponent.

(d) In the event of an injury, the Referee may require a player to continue play or concede the match, except where the injury is contributed to by his opponent, or where it was caused by dangerous play on the part of the opponent. In the former case, the Referee may allow time for the injured player to receive attention and recover, and in the latter, the injured player shall be awarded the match under Rule 19 (d) (ii).

(e) In the event of the ball breaking, a new ball may be knocked-up, as provided for in Rule 15 (b).

Note to Referees (i) In allowing time for a player to receive attention and recover, the Referee should ensure that there is no conflict with the obligation of a player to comply with Rule 16 (b), that is, that the effects of the injury are not exaggerated and used as an excuse to recover strength or wind. (ii) The Referee should not interpret the words 'contributed to by his opponent' to include the situation where the injury to the player is a result of that player occupying an unneccessarily close position to his opponent. (iii) The practice of serving faults deliberately to obtain an additional period of rest is contrary to the spirit of the game and Rule 16 (b). When the Referee is satisfied that a player is doing so, he shall, after warning him in terms of Rule 16 (b), award the game to his opponent.

17 CONTROL OF A MATCH A match is normally controlled by a Referee, assisted by a Marker. One person may be appointed to carry out the functions of both Referee and Marker. When a decision has been made by a Referee, he shall announce it to the players and the Marker shall repeat it with the subsequent score. Up to one hour before the commencement of a match either player may request a Referee and/or a Marker other than appointed, and this request may be considered and a substitute appointed. Players are not permitted to request any such change after the commencement of a match, unless both agree to do so. In either case the decision as to whether an official is to be replaced or not must remain in the hands of the Tournament Referee, where applicable.

18 DUTIES OF MARKER
(a) The Marker calls the play and the score, with the server's score first. He shall call 'Foot-Fault', 'Fault', 'Not-up', 'Out', or 'Down' as appropriate.

(b) If in the course of play the Marker calls 'Not-up', 'Out', or 'Down' or in the case of a second service, 'Foot-Fault', or 'Fault', then the rally shall cease.

(c) If the Marker's decision is reversed on appeal, a Let shall be allowed, except as provided for in Rules 11 (b) (iii) and (iv) and 19

(b) (iv) and (v).

(d) Any service or return shall be considered good unless otherwise called.

(e) After the server has served a fault, which has not been taken, the Market shall repeat the score and add the words 'One fault', before the server serves again. This call will be repeated should subsequent rallies end in a Let, until the stroke is finally decided.

(f) When no Referee is appointed, the Marker shall exercise all the powers of the Referee.

(g) If the Marker is unsighted or uncertain, he shall call on the Referee to make the relevant decision; if the latter is unable to do so, a Let shall be allowed.

19 DUTIES OF REFEREE

(a) The Referee shall award Lets and Strokes and make decisions where called for by the Rules, and shall decide all appeals, including those against the Marker's calls and decisions. The decision of the Referee shall be final.

(b) He shall in no way intervene in the Marker's calling except: (i) upon appeal by one of the players. (ii) as provided for in Rule 12. (iii) when it is evident that the score has been incorrectly called, in which case he should draw the Marker's attention to the fact. (iv) when the Marker has failed to call the ball 'Not up', 'Out', or 'Down' and, on appeal, he rules that such was in fact the case, the stroke should be awarded accordingly. (v) when the Marker has called 'Not up', 'Out', or 'Down' and, on appeal, he rules that this was not the case, a Let shall be allowed except that, if in the Referee's opinion the Marker's call had interrupted an undoubted winning return, he shall award the stroke accordingly. (vi) if he is certain that the Marker has made an obvious error in stopping play or allowing play to continue, he shall immediately rule accordingly.

(c) The Referee is responsible that all times laid down in the Rules are strictly adhered to.

(d) In exceptional cases, the Referee may order: (i) a player, who has left the court, to play on. (ii) a player to leave the court and to award the match to the opponent. (iii) a match to be awarded to a player whose opponent fails to be present on court within 10 minutes of the advertised time of play. (iv) play to be stopped in order to warn that the conduct of one or both of the players is leading to an infringement of the Rules. A Referee should avail himself of this Rule as early as possible when either player is showing a tendency to break the provisions of Rule 12.

(e) If after a warning a player continues to contravene Rule 15 (c) the Referee shall award a game to the opponent.

Appendix I: Definitions
COURT MARKINGS
Board or Tin The expression denoting a band, the top of which is
0.48m (19 inches) from the floor across the lower part of the front
wall above which the ball must be returned before the stroke is good.
Cut Line A line upon the front wall, the top edge of which is
1.83m (6 feet) above the floor and extending the full width of the
court.
Half-Court Line A line set out upon the floor parallel to the side
walls, dividing the back half of the court into two equal parts.
Short Line A line set out upon the floor parallel to and 5.49m (18
feet) from the front wall and extending the full width of the court.
Quarter Court One part of the back half of the court behind the
short line which has been divided into two equal parts by the
half-court line.
Service Box or Box A square delimited area in each quarter court
from which hand-in serves.

GENERAL
Hand The period from the time when a player becomes hand-in
until he becomes hand-out.
Hand-in The player who serves.
Hand-out The player who receives service.
Point A point is won by the player who is hand-in and who wins a
stroke.
Striker The player whose turn it is to play after the ball has hit the
front wall.
Stroke A stroke is won by the player whose opponent fails to serve
or make a good return in accordance with the rules.

THE MARKERS CALLS
Fault The service is a fault.
Foot-fault The service is a foot-fault.
One Fault The server is serving the second service.
Hand-out The server has served his hand out, or lost the rally and
so ceases to be hand-in.
Down The ball has been struck against the tin or board.
Not-up The ball has not been served or returned above the board
in accordance with the rules.
Out The ball has touched the front, sides or back of the court
above the area prepared for play or has passed over any cross bars
or other part of the roof of the court. The lines delineating such
area, the lighting equipment and the roof are out.
Let Ball The call made by the referee and repeated by the marker
to indicate that a rally should be replayed.
No Let The call made by the referee and repeated by the marker to

indicate that an appeal has been refused.

Stroke to . . . The call made by the referee and repeated by the marker when the referee has awarded a stroke to a player.

No Set The game is to be played to 9 points after the score has reached 8-8.

Set Two The game is to be played to 10 points after the score has reached 8-8.

Game Ball The server requires one point to win the game.

Match Ball The server requires one point to win the match.

Stop Stop play.

Ten Seconds There are 10 seconds remaining before the start of the next game.

THE REFEREE'S CALLS

Let Ball The rally should be replayed.

No Let An appeal has been refused.

Stroke to . . . The stroke has been awarded to a player.

Stop Stop play.

Time Start play.

Appendix II: Dimensions of a Singles Court

Length: 9.75m (32 feet): Breadth: 6.40m (21 feet)

Height to upper edge of cut line on front wall: 1.83m (6 feet)

Height to lower edge of front-wall line: 4.57m (15 feet)

Height to lower edge of back-wall line: 2.13m (7 feet)

Distance to further edge of short line from front-wall: 5.49m (18 feet)

Height to upper edge of board from ground: 0.48m (19 inches)

Thickness of board (flat or rounded at top): 12.5mm to 25mm (½ to 1 inch)

Height of side-wall line: The diagonal line joining the front-wall line and the back-wall line.

The service boxes shall be entirely enclosed on 3 sides within the court by lines, the short line forming the side nearest to the front-wall, the side-wall bounding the fourth side.

The internal dimensions of the service boxes shall be 1.60m (5ft 3in).

All dimensions in the court shall be measured, where practicable, from the junction of the floor and front wall, at a height of 1m above the finished floor.

All lines of the court shall be 50mm (2 inches) in width and all lines shall be coloured red. In respect of the outer boundary lines on the walls, it is suggested that the plaster should be so shaped as to produce a concave channel along such lines.

Appendix III: Specification of a Racket
1 DIMENSIONS
Maximum length: 685mm (27 ins)
Internal stringing
Maximum length: 215mm (8.5 ins)
Maximum breadth: 184mm (7.25 ins)
Framework of head
Maximum width across the face: 14mm (0.56 ins)
Minimum width across the face: 9mm (0.36 ins)
Maximum depth across the face: 20mm (0.81 ins)
Minimum depth across the face: 12mm (0.47 ins)
Shaft
Minimum thickness: 9mm (0.36 ins)
Maximum weight (including stringing and bumper strip): 255gms (9 oz)

2 CONSTRUCTION
At all times, the head or shaft shall not contain edges with a radius of curvature less than 2mm. Strings and string ends must be recessed within the racket head or, in cases where such recessing is impractical because of the racket material, or design, must be protected by a non-marking and securely attached bumper strip made of a flexible material, which cannot crease into sharp edges following abrasive contact with floors or walls. Strings shall be gut, nylon or a substitute material, providing metal is not used. Only two layers of string shall be allowed and these shall be alternately interlaced to form an orthogonal array.
Note to Referees on Degradation
Rackets which have suffered damage so as to cause a potential hazard must not be used for play, unless the damaged region is repaired adhesively or by wound overlays, such that the damaged region becomes stronger than the material on either side of the damaged zone and has a smooth surface.

Appendix IV: Specification for Squash Racket Balls
The ball must conform to the following:
1 It must weigh not less than 23.3 grammes and not more than 24.6 grammes (approximately 360-380 grains).
2 Its diameter must be not less than 39.5mm and not more than 41.5mm (approximately 1.56 to 1.63 inches).
3 It must have a surface finish which guarantees continuing correct rebound.
4 It must be of type specifically approved for championship play by the ISRF.
5 Compression Specification: (i) The ball is mounted in an apparatus and a load of 0.5kgm is applied which deforms the ball slightly

Subsequent deformation in the test is measured from this datum. (ii) An additional load of 2.4kgm is applied and this deforms the ball further. The deformation from the datum position is recorded. (iii) The deformation obtained in (ii) should be between 3 and 7mm for balls of playing properties acceptable to the ISRF.

Appendix V: Colour of Players' Clothing
Organisers may specify regulations concerning players' clothing which must be complied with in their particular tournament or tournaments.

SRA Note For all events under the control of the SRA, players are required to wear white and/or light matching pastel clothing during the course of play. A coloured trim with a maximum width of 50mm (2 inches) is permissible. Shoes should be predominantly white with only 20% of colour trim inclusive of sole, which must be non marking. The maximum area for advertising is 50mm^2 (2 square inches). Member countries of the ISRF have a limited discretion to allow advertising of a greater size to be worn for any other events under their control. The Referee's decision on compliance shall be final.

Note Footwear is deemed clothing.

The Doubles Game
1 SIDES Sides shall consist of two players each.

2 SCORE Every point won by either side shall add one to its score.

3 GAME The game shall be 15 up. That is, the side which first scores 15 points wins the game, excepting that:
(a) At 13-all the side which first reached the score 13 must elect one of the following before making the next serve: (i) Set to 5 points, making the game 18 points; (ii) Set to 3 points, making the game 16 points; (iii) No set, in which case the game remains at 15 points.
(b) At 14-all, provided the score has not been 13-all, the side which first reached the score of 14 must elect one of the following before the next serve: (i) Set to 3 points, making the game 17 points: (ii) No set, in which case the game remains at 15 points.

4 MATCH In all tournaments sanctioned by the Association matches shall be for the best three out of five games.

5 SERVER At the start of a match the choice to serve or receive shall be decided by the spin of a racket.
The two partners of a side shall serve in succession, the first

retaining his serve until his side has lost a point. When the side has lost the next point, the side shall be declared out and the serve revert to the opponents. On the first serve of every game, however, the 'in' side shall be declared 'out' after it has lost one point only.

The order of serving within a side shall not be changed during the progress of a game.

At the end of a game the side which has won that game shall have the choice of serving or receiving to begin the next game.

6 SERVICE A ball is in play from the moment at which it is delivered in service (unless a fault or a let) and remains in play until the point is decided.

At the beginning of each game and each time a side becomes 'in' the ball shall be served from whichever service box the first server for the side elects and thereafter alternately until the side is 'out' or until the end of the game. If the server serves from the wrong box there shall be no penalty and the service shall count and the play shall proceed as if the box served from was the correct box, except that, if the receiver does not attempt to return the service, he may demand that it be served from the other box, or, if before the receiver attempts to return the service the referee calls a let, the service shall be made from the other box.

The server, until the ball has left the racket from the service, must stand with at least one foot on the floor within and not touching the line surrounding the service box and serve the ball on to the front wall above the cut line and below the out-of-court line before it touches any other part of the court, so that on its rebound (return) it first strikes the floor within, but not touching, the lines of the opposite service court, either before or after touching any other wall or walls within the court. Otherwise it is a fault.

If it be the first fault, the server shall serve again from the same side. If the server make two consecutive faults, he loses that point.

7 RETURN OF SERVICE AND SUBSEQUENT PLAY
(a) At the beginning of each game each side shall designate one of its players to receive service in the right-hand service court and the other to receive service in the left-hand service court and throughout the course of such game the service must be received by the player so designated.
(b) To make a good return the ball must be struck on the volley or before it has touched the floor twice and reached the front wall on the fly above the tell-tale and it may touch any wall or walls within the court before or after reaching the front wall.
(c) If the designated receiver fails to make a good return of a good service it is a point for the serving side. If the designated receiver makes a good return of service the side shall alternate making

returns until one side fails to make a good return. A failure to make a good return is a point for the other side.

(d) A service called a fault may not be played, but the receiver may volley any service which has struck the front wall in accordance with rule 6.

(e) Until the ball has been touched or has hit the floor twice, it may be struck at any number of times by either or both players on a side.

(f) If at any time the ball hits outside the playing surfaces of the court, which includes the ceiling and/or lights or beams, or hits a line marking the playing surfaces of the court (except on the first service, when it is one fault), it is a point against the side so hitting the ball.

8 LET A let is the stopping of play and the playing over of the point. The following are lets which are not definitely covered in other rules and a let shall be called:

(a) If, on the first bounce from the floor, the ball hits on or above the back wall line.

(b) If either player on the striking side is inadvertently hindered by either of his opponents from reaching or striking at the ball.

(c) If, owing to the position of either of his opponents, a player is unable to avoid being touched by a ball.

(d) If either player on the striking side refrains from striking at the ball owing to a reasonable fear of injuring one of his opponents.

(e) If, in the act of striking and before hitting the ball, the striker's racket is touched by either of his opponents or either of their rackets, even though the striker completes the stroke. However, play continues unless the let has been called by the marker. It is the duty of the marker to call a let, immediately stopping the play.

Notes to Referees

No let shall be allowed on any strokes a player makes unless: (i) In the act of striking and before hitting the ball he touches or is touched by one of his opponents or his racket. (ii) The striker could have made a good return. Each player on the striking side is entitled to make a return so long as the ball is still in play and is entitled to a let within the above definitions even if his partner has struck at the ball and missed it completely or if he himself has struck at the ball and missed it completely, but still has an opportunity to play it.

9 KEEPING OUT OF OPPONENTS' WAY Each player must get out of his opponent's way immediately after he has struck the ball and do all he can to:

(a) Give his opponents a fair view of the ball. However, interference purely with an adversary's vision in following the flight of the ball is no let.

(b) Avoid interfering with either opponent in getting to and/or striking at the ball.
(c) Leave both opponents, as far as possible, free to play the ball to any part of the front wall or to either wall near the front wall.

10 BAULK If in the opinion of the marker interference with the striker is unnecessary, it shall constitute a baulk. When a baulk is called, the play shall stop and the point go to side interfered with. Unnecessary crowding shall constitute a baulk, even though the opposing player is not actually prevented from reaching the ball or striking at it. It is the duty of the referee to call a baulk, immediately stopping the play.

11 FAIR BALL TOUCHING PLAYERS If a fair ball, after hitting the front wall and before being played again, touches any player or anything he wears or carries, before touching the floor twice, the side of the player touched loses the point.

12 FAIRLY STRUCK BALL HITTING PLAYER
(a) If the ball after being struck from a good service or a good return and before reaching the front wall, hits one of the striker's opponents or his racket or anything he wears or carries: (i) It shall be a let if the ball strikes the front wall fairly or would have done so but for such interference. (ii) If the return would not have been good, the striker's side shall lose the point. (iii) The marker shall decide as to (i) or (ii).
(b) When a fairly struck ball hits the striker's partner, it is a point for the other side.

13 PLAYER'S PRIVILEGE IN CASE OF LET OR BAULK If the marker fails to call a let or baulk, when in the opinion of the player he has been interfered with, the player may appeal to the marker.

14 KNOCK-UP At the request of either side the referee shall allow to either side or to the two sides together a period of five minutes during the hour preceding the start of a match for knocking-up in the court in which a match is to be played. The right to knock-up first shall be decided by the spin of a racket.

15 CONTINUITY OF PLAY Play shall be continuous from the first service until the match is concluded except that between the third and fourth games play may be suspended by any player for a period not to exceed five minutes and except that, when necessitated by circumstances not within the control of the players the marker may suspend play for such a period as he may consider necessary.

This proviso shall be strictly construed and play shall never be suspended to allow a player to recover his strength or his wind. The marker shall be the sole judge of intentional delay and, after giving warning, he must disqualify the offender.

16 (a) No ball, before or during a match, may be artificially treated; that is, heated or chilled.
(b) At any time when not in actual play another ball may be substituted by the mutual consent of the players or by decision of the marker.

17 REFEREE The referee's decisions on all questions shall be final. The referee has power to order:
(a) A player who has left the court to play on.
(b) A player to leave the court for any reason whatsoever and may award the match to his opponents.
(c) A match to be awarded to a player whose opponent fails to be present in the court within ten minutes of the advertised time of play.